JOHN PEEL

JOHN PEEL

A Life in Music

MICHAEL HEATLEY

MICHAEL O'MARA BOOKS LIMITED

First published in Great Britain in 2004 by
Michael O'Mara Books Limited
9 Lion Yard, Tremadoc Road
London sw4 7nq

Michael O'Mara Books Limited paperback edition
first published in 2005

A CIP catalogue record for this book is available
from the British Library

ISBN 1-84317-157-0

3 5 7 9 10 8 6 4

www.mombooks.com

Designed and typeset by Martin Bristow

Printed and bound in England
by Cox & Wyman Ltd, Reading, Berks

Contents

Author's Acknowledgements

This book was very much a team effort, so the author would like to thank writers/researchers Nigel Cross, Alan Kinsman, Graham Betts and Ian Shirley for valued assistance on specific chapters where their knowledge was superior to mine.

Also Nephele Headleand, Deke Leonard, Ayden Peach, Chris Heatley, John Tobler, Pete Frame and Rose Lucas. And lastly Kate Gribble, Helen Cumberbatch, Lindsay Davies, Toby Buchan, Chris Maynard, Judy Palmer and all at Michael O'Mara Books.

Photograph Acknowledgements

Page 1: Getty Images (*above*), SIPA/Rex Features (*below*); page 2: Mirrorpix (*above*), LFI (*below*); page 3: PA Photos (*below*), Popperfoto.com (*above*); page 4: Getty Images (*above*), Rex Features (*below*); page 5: Jeff Spicer/Alpha (*left*), PA Photos (*right*); page 6: Mirrorpix (*both*); page 7: Mirrorpix (*above*), Alastair Indge/Retna (*below*); page 8: Popperfoto.com (*above*), PA Photos (*below*); page 9: LF/LFI (*above*), Jeff Albertson/Corbis (*inset*), Graham Wright/Rex Features (*below*); page 10: Everett Collection/Rex Features (*above left*), Skyline/Rex Features (*above right*), Richard Young/Rex Features (*below*); page 11: Paul Slattery/Retna (*above*), Andre Csillag/Rex Features (*below*); page 12: John Rogers/Rex Features (*above*), RIP/Retna (*below*); page 13: PA Photos (*above*), Topfoto/UPPA (*below*); page 14: PA Photos (*above*), Rex Features (*below*); page 15: Bryn Colton/Assignments Photographers/Corbis (*above*), PA Photos (*below*); page 16: Topfoto.

Introduction

WHEN SHADOWS GUITARIST Hank Marvin, the man whose Fender Stratocastering launched innumerable rock'n'roll careers, was nominated to receive the OBE in 2004 after four and a half decades in music, he decided to decline the offer 'for personal and private reasons'. Six years earlier, however, veteran DJ John Peel had accepted the prestigious award with alacrity.

The pair, axeman and disc-spinner, have arguably had a similarly seismic effect on the musical tastes of the British nation. Yet though Peel became inextricably linked with the punk movement that he did so much to foster in the mid-1970s – and before that was a prominent and enthusiastic supporter of the 1960s hippie counter-culture – he was, paradoxically, something of a traditionalist. Indeed, his first choice when invited on to Radio Four's *Desert Island Discs* was Handel's 'Zadok the Priest' as played at the coronation of George VI, a tune he admitted always brought a tear to his eye.

Perhaps it was the fact that the King only took the throne reluctantly (more than two years before Peel's birth) after his brother's sudden abdication, and had overcome a stammer to become an eloquent speaker, that retrospectively impressed. For Peel was himself a shy man, and overcame his natural reticence by visualizing a listener modelled on himself. Perhaps this was why he remained such a unique communicator forty years after his broadcasting career began.

Born John Robert Parker Ravenscroft at the beginning of the Second World War, he was in his mid-teens when Elvis Presley unleashed his primeval rock'n'roll on an unsuspecting world, and so was in an ideal position to witness the growth of the most potent force in youth culture. He would soon pursue that force to its very source, the United States, where he would begin his career as a broadcaster and musical tastemaker. A short spell aboard ship as a 'pirate' on Radio London was followed by an invitation to join Radio One – the place where the vast majority of his listeners would have first encountered him – as a founder DJ. At his death he was the only survivor of the original twenty-nine Radio One DJs who was still broadcasting for the station, having enjoyed uninterrupted service since 1967 – even if he was now working the 'midnight shift'.

Everyone has their own John Peel story, taking in everything from his regular habit of playing records at the wrong speed to providing people with their own personal 'road to Damascus' revelation akin to his own with Presley's 'Heartbreak Hotel'. Some of the tributes from fellow broadcasters and musicians have been gathered as an appendix to this book. Yet it was his listeners, not the stars, that concerned John Peel. Few of the groups and artists to whom he gave airtime ever even met the man. Like his listeners, though, they felt they knew him well.

Peel's long-time producer John Walters was once heard to say: 'If Peel ever hits puberty we're in real trouble.' The DJ was sixty-five when he departed this earth, but in many ways he never did grow up. There are many rock stars taken too early who can also claim that distinction – but by retaining an almost childlike passion for music, John Peel's influence in helping countless listeners reach their own musical maturity was monumental. We all owe him for that.

MICHAEL HEATLEY
Hampshire, November 2004

I

A Cheshire Childhood

JOHN RAVENSCROFT WAS BORN on 30 August 1939, into a world that was, for the second time that century, in the shadow of storm clouds. Two days later the evacuation of UK cities would begin, kids clutching their personal possessions in one hand and gas masks in the other as they prepared to face life miles from home in unfamiliar surroundings. On 3 September, two days after Hitler's invasion of Poland, Britain declared war against Germany, and thus the country was plunged into conflict once again.

Not that this would impinge upon young Master Ravenscroft's existence until some years later. He was born and brought up in Burton, a small village on the edge of the River Dee, in the Wirral, the 'posh' side of the Mersey from the port of Liverpool – which, unsurprisingly, would bear the brunt of much Luftwaffe bombing. One of his earliest childhood memories dates from the age of four when he and younger brother Francis went to a part of the garden into which they'd been forbidden to venture: 'It was roughly the

John Peel: A Life in Music

size and shape of a football pitch, as I recall, with a path that ran effectively along the halfway line. On this occasion I went up there and I said to Francis, "I'm going to go into the top half of the garden," and he expressed disapproval, [though] he probably couldn't even speak at the time.

'Showing the bravery of an older brother, I stepped into the top half of the garden, and as I did, a German plane flew over – we recognized it from the black crosses on the wings. So I thought, "Whatever I've been told is right – I *mustn't* go into the top half of the garden" – and barely went in for the whole of the rest of the time that we lived there as a consequence.'

Obedience was the order of the day, since father Robert and mother Joan appear to have been very much distant figures who inspired awe and respect as much as love. John's father was a prosperous industrialist who had made his money from the cotton trade, running the family firm, but who willingly joined up to fight the enemy – and was posted to North Africa for his trouble. So patriotic was he that there was a flagpole outside the house from which John claimed the Union Jack was flown throughout the whole of the war, though pictorial evidence fails to back this up.

Another early wartime memory finds John standing in one of the upstairs bedrooms and looking over to where Birkenhead and Liverpool were burning: 'It was the middle of the night, I was aware of that, but it looked as though the sun had just gone down – there was a big red glow in the sky.'

Like so many war babies, John and Francis, two years his junior, saw very little of their father until the end of hostilities when he was demobbed and returned to 'civvy street': 'In my head, I never saw my dad at all until I was six years old.' Talking on the Anglia TV show *Going Home* in 2002, John recalled a touching and unusual reunion. 'One afternoon,

Francis and I were playing in the garden. We heard a motorbike coming down the road, and rushed out to watch it go by, but it didn't go by; the rider signalled for a left turn, and turned into the driveway, which was a kind of gravel driveway round a central piece of grass. I ran into the house and upstairs to where my mother was washing her hair in the sink – there was a window overlooking the driveway – and I said to her, "Mummy, Mummy, there's a funny-looking man at the door." She looked out of the window and, as I remember it, she burst into tears and said, "That's your father." So I rushed back downstairs again and told Francis, and we just stood there, looking at him and thinking, as he took off his motorcycling gear, "So *that's* what a father looks like."'

Another son, Alan, was born after the end of the war, seven years John's junior ('He was clearly my dad's favourite, which is fair enough because he knew him a lot better'), but their parents were subsequently to divorce. It has been said that his less than satisfactory home life as a child, combined with a disastrous first marriage of his own, made John appreciate all the more the domestic happiness he enjoyed in the last three decades of his life with second wife Sheila and his four children – two sons and two daughters.

When he guested on BBC Radio Four's *Desert Island Discs* in 1989, John opened up with some rare feelings about his father, who had died about fifteen years previously. 'He was a cotton broker in a family business which my grandfather had been involved in and probably others before that,' he reflected, 'but it was a dying business . . . a lot of people had kept it going through the war, but he'd gone off and fought in North Africa and so forth, so the family business had been in suspension for about five years. When he came back it was quite difficult to get going again – it lasted his lifetime, but it wasn't the sort of business which he'd have passed on to us.

'I miss him now more then when he actually died,' he continued, 'because there are more things now which have happened that I'd have liked him to have known about – doing this programme being one of them, but things like honorary degrees and so forth. When I started on Radio One he'd go into his club, the Old Hall Club in Liverpool, with a lot of stories which would start: "You'll never guess what that damn fool boy of mine has done now!" But he used to tell people and I was quite pleased with that, because he obviously saw me as a bad lot at one stage.'

His mother (who changed her name from Joan to Harriet some time during the 1960s, and sent printed cards to friends and acquaintances informing them of the fact) seems not to have filled the emotional vacuum in young John's life, preferring to leave the day-to-day running of the household in the more than capable hands of a nanny, Miss Florence Horn. The latter rejoiced in the nickname of 'Trader' Horn, after the famous sea captain of the Victorian era, and, as John admits, she was 'the person around whom our lives revolved'. So affectionate were his memories that he named his younger daughter Florence in her memory, though the name is always commuted to 'Flossie'.

'My mother used to spend a lot of time in her bedroom reading romantic fiction – she would say "superior romantic fiction" – and we were raised by Trader. We used to have those awful conversations – who would you rather died, Mum or Trader? And invariably we used to say my mother because Trader was just so warm and protecting . . . And she had a range of sisters and friends in Liverpool who could secretly become friends of yours as well; they were people that you know, but your parents didn't know. They all had wonderful names which people don't have any more. I mean, how long is it since you met a Phyllis?'

Discipline was administered parentally. 'I remember standing at the bottom of the staircase with Nanny, waiting for my mother to come down and beat me. The routine was that Trader would go and stand at the bottom of the stairs and shout the fateful words, "Are you there?" My mother would be in her bedroom and I'd be standing at the bottom of the stairs straining my ears to hear what was going on. If she did hear Trader calling she'd come swooping like one of the Furies out of her bedroom, grab a belt as she flung herself down the stairs and, no questions asked, take me into the dining room, put me over the table and give me a bit of a hiding. Not a happy memory . . .

'The only time my father beat me, which he did in a very formal kind of old-fashioned way, he gave me a good talking-to and then, with his captain's swagger stick, he gave me four strokes on my backside; that didn't help our relationship, I'll be honest. My mother, on the other hand, was a great enthusiast for . . . corporal punishment; she stopped just short of capital punishment, thank God!' At the end of the day, he felt that, though she was an amazing woman, she had not been a great mother. 'You need somebody into whose arms you can fling yourself when distressed, and she certainly wasn't that kind of mother at all.'

Perhaps, John told the *Glasgow Herald*'s Teddy Jamieson in a revealing interview six months before his death, his mother's reserve came from being an only child, whose own mother had died when she was just a year old. 'It's a *Home Truths* story,' he explained. 'The only picture she had of her mother, Ethel Parker, was a silhouette of the type which used to be quite popular on piers. A few years before my mum died, some aunt gave her a photograph of Ethel Parker – and she never looked at it . . . because she just couldn't bear, that late in life, discovering [that] her mum wasn't how she'd always imagined her to be.' In the end, he summed up his parents as 'both probably quite nice people – but fucked-up, as people are'.

John's pre-school days were spent in a fashion he admits 'would be described by today's young people as fantastically dull. You'd spend most of the time pottering around the garden, devising your own little fantasy world, which I think is probably quite good for people to do. [We] used to spend a lot of time sitting in a tree, which we used to call the horse and cart tree, which overlooked the adjoining lane. Old Mr Bettens used to come down, presumably to catch the bus which stopped outside our house, and would give us apples and sweets and things in a way that would be very much disapproved of now. But he was a nice old fella, and we used to sit in that tree for hours in the hope that he would come by.'

Privately owned cars were the exception rather than the rule in those days, but the well-to-do Bob Ravenscroft was something of an enthusiast – and it was a taste his eldest son caught from an early age. 'My dad had some rather exotic cars: a Citroën Traction Avant, a Morgan three-wheeler and a Minerva. A couple of my father's sisters were really into vintage cars – when they were just old cars – and one of them took me to the hill climb at Shelsley Walsh in a Bugatti that had belonged to Malcolm Campbell. And at one time, two of the three Talbot 105s that were built for a race at Brooklands were in my family.'

As a young boy John had problems with wetting the bed, an all-too-frequent event that would be preceded by dreams of cycling into a pond that could be seen over the Ravenscrofts' fence. 'It happened so often that I kind of knew, even while I was dreaming, what was going to happen, and I would desperately try to throw myself off the bicycle to avoid the wet bed and the recriminations that were going to occur.' He also managed to ride his tricycle through the side of the greenhouse, cutting his left arm quite badly in a couple of places and leaving lifelong scars. The wounds were stitched up by the local doctor on the dining-room table, and John remained proud of the fact that he didn't cry during the course of the operation: 'This kind of gave me an identity, and I thought to myself that "I'm the boy who doesn't cry" . . . I never cried again for about another twenty to twenty-two years.'

Music had yet to make an impact on the young John Ravenscroft: in fact, he didn't remember music being played at home in any form, although his father had a collection of dance-band records from the 1930s that he passed on to his son: 'I think I used to be given records by despairing relatives – "What shall we give the boy?" – and I just liked them as objects. I still do.'

John's first educational port of call at the age of seven was across the border at Woodlands Preparatory School, Deganwy, North Wales, where naked cold-water baths first thing each morning were the order of the day. But, as the establishment's name suggested, he was destined for bigger and better things. The start of the 1950s saw him dispatched far from Trader's embrace to Shrewsbury School in Shropshire, a major public (fee-paying) school, where his father hoped that John's rough edges would be rubbed off and a suitable son and heir emerge. Earlier attempts to make him conform, including making him join 'a kind of middle-class football club called the Liverpool Ramblers, where everybody dressed in cavalry-twill trousers and suede shoes, sports jackets and knitted ties,' had come to naught. He'd dutifully gone along and played a couple of times 'and absolutely *hated* it . . . because it was something that my parents and their friends and the people that I was supposed to want to associate with [would approve of]'.

The same rebellious streak was soon to make itself clear at Shrewsbury, where John was two years below the star trio of comic Peter Cook, satirist and future *Private Eye* editor Richard Ingrams and campaigning left-wing journalist Paul Foot, whose politics he shared. (*Monty Python* actor-turned-world traveller Michael Palin was also a contemporary, though some three years Peel's junior.)

Peel was a shy boy who tended towards obstinate non-conformity, for which he paid in regular thrashings – he recalled that the school authorities 'practically had to wake [me] up during the night in order to administer the required number of sound beatings'. Peel estimated the 'flagellation rate' in his first term at once every three days, but denied having been scarred by these experiences. 'You developed techniques for coping,' he reflected.

More sinister was what today we would term sexual harassment. Predatory older boys would target younger pupils, and, as John would later recall, 'In the absence of women of any sort at all they turned to cute boys as a kind of stopgap measure.' This category, it seems, included him: 'When I was thirteen I was rather lovely, and much sought-after by older boys who, if they developed an appetite for you, could have you beaten on a number of pretexts. Several of them have gone on to achieve positions of some eminence in the financial world,' he continued. 'I'm sometimes tempted to turn up with a little rouge on my cheeks and say, "I'm ready for you now, my angel" to some ageing captain of industry.' Little surprise, then, that he eventually sought an escape route from reality – in music.

Academic pursuits soon began to pale in comparison to the development of his alternative new interest. Even in those pre-rock'n'roll days, Peel was keen to share his enthusiasm with others and evangelize about the new world he'd discovered. Artists whose music he was buying in the 1950s included the non-threatening likes of Frankie Laine, Doris Day, Winifred Atwell, Johnnie Ray and Guy Mitchell. The school jazz club, known as High Society, seemed a likely place in which to find kindred spirits, but in reality was populated by narrow-minded snobs who, while happy to listen to revered New Orleans trombonist Kid Ory, sneered at John's prized 78 rpm record of Oklahoma saxophonist Earl Bostic, a man from a more recent era without the 'credibility' of his rival, Ory.

Rejected, but far from unbowed ('I knew I was right, I'm an opinionated bugger!'), John turned to a one-on-one relationship with his radio. It was clearly a pointer to the rest of his life. 'From then on,' he reflected later, 'I wanted to play records on the radio to people who ought to share them.' The use of 'ought' in that sentence is indicative of the man's missionary zeal.

By and large, John didn't enjoy the company of fellow Salopians. 'The senior boys at school that I was supposed to admire and emulate were . . . complete pricks,' he once stated flatly. The value system into which he was being indoctrinated was 'meaningless to me, if not actively unpleasant', and he grew ever more frustrated.

Another outlet, parallel to his growing interest in music, was association football. Quite apart from the public-school rugby-playing tradition, it was considered somewhat common to follow a professional football team, which made the young Ravenscroft's love of Liverpool FC all the stronger. Liverpool had been the first team to win the First Division title – the ultimate domestic prize at the time – after League football was resumed in time for the 1946–47 season. Perhaps it was this that first kick-started John's love affair with the team from the red half of the city, though as

Everton had won the last League title before the war, perhaps John would have been a fan of the Blues had he been born five or six years earlier.

But those relative fortunes were to change during John's spell at Shrewsbury: in 1954, the teams would pass each other as Liverpool were relegated and Everton regained the top-flight status they continue to enjoy to this day. While most fans from the city come from 'red' or 'blue' families, Peel's allegiance had no such tribal roots. He later confessed that his love of the Reds was 'cemented by the knowledge that only proletarian folk supported a professional football team . . . the more people that told me that, the more interested I became.' This would, of course, grow into a lifelong passion.

As any Harry Potter reader will surely know, the public-school system was and is run on a 'house' basis, the housemaster being the surrogate father to all those under his care. So if the young Ravenscroft couldn't find much solace in his fellow pupils, he was fortunate in having a sympathetic man as his housemaster. This was Mr (later the Reverend) R. H. J. Brooke, to whom Peel was – even just before his death – sincerely intending to dedicate his autobiography. 'At a time when the school was being encouraged to produce people to run the Empire and Daddy's business,' he told *Record Collector*'s Mark Paytress, 'he encouraged me just to be myself and do what I wanted to do. He tried to channel my natural instincts into something constructive. And I think in a way he succeeded. He recognized uniquely that I was a fairly hopeless case academically, but encouraged me in some of my more wayward pursuits . . . he rather liked the idea of having a disruptive influence in the house.'

Rather than make John suffer Chopin's piano études, Brooke put his charge into a study next to the library, where he could play his Lonnie Donegan records without let or hindrance. Donegan was the high priest of skiffle, the homespun blend of folk, jazz, gospel and blues that predated British rock'n'roll. And though the housemaster wasn't interested in skiffle himself, he did, John reflected later, 'approve of the principle behind it'.

Donegan was, of course, a legendary figure who changed the face of British popular music. His breakthrough recording of Leadbelly's 'Rock Island Line', made while he was a member of Chris Barber's Jazz Band, sold over 3 million copies and made the Top Ten in both Britain and the States in 1956. 'Rock Island Line' was to be one of the two key records in the young John Ravenscroft's life. And he wasn't alone. Away from the confines of Shrewsbury School, Peel's fellow Merseysiders Paul McCartney and John Lennon both became equally gripped by the gospel of skiffle.

As ever, though, the major musical breakthroughs were happening several thousand miles away across the Atlantic. Before John discovered the American Forces Network, the only way of catching the latest sounds was good old 'Auntie' BBC. On radio shows such as *Housewives' Choice*, broadcast on what was then called the Light Programme, a teenager could listen for hours . . . and still not hear anything he liked. John subscribed to *New Musical Express*, a music newspaper founded in 1952 and still going strong today, and had read that a young man by the name of Elvis Presley had been knocking 'em dead in the States. Presley was described as 'a mixture of Billy Daniels and Johnnie Ray', which made the Merseyside teenager even more keen to investigate.

It was on the Beeb's *Two-Way Family Favourites*, hosted by Jean Metcalfe and Cliff Michelmore, that John first heard Elvis. The modus operandi of the show, which at its peak enjoyed an audience of 16 million in Britain alone, was to reunite 'our boys overseas' with their families at home – and remember that, in these years where rationing was still a very recent memory, continental Europe was awash with Allied troops. A request was made for a record by 'new American singing sensation' Elvis Presley, and for sixteen-year-old John Ravenscroft the genie was well and truly out of the bottle.

'Heartbreak Hotel' was the song. 'It sounds idiotic to say it now,' Peel told Radio One book author Simon Garfield in 1998 – four decades having done little or nothing to dim the memory – 'but it was a revelation, just like being transported to another planet. The only thing that came close was when I heard Little Richard a few weeks later. It was genuinely frightening . . .'

During school holidays, John attempted in vain to convert brother Francis to the gospel of rock'n'roll. 'I was accumulating records at quite a rate,' he recalled many years later, 'and, living in the country, I had no one I could play them to except my brother, and he wasn't interested – and also I was fired by parental disapproval. My father would stick his head in and say "What's that *awful* record you're playing there?" and would mispronounce the names of the artists deliberately to inflame [me] further – and I thought, "What I'd really like is a job on the radio playing records that I like to other people" – and that, in essence, is all I've ever done. People try to read more into it than that, but there isn't any more to it.'

Not long after his Elvis epiphany, he discovered American Forces Network radio – which broadcast to US troops who were based in Europe to keep the post-war peace, but which was meat and drink to a music-hungry schoolboy desperate to hear Chicago blues and the exotic sounds of the South. Besides, the ratio of worthwhile music was immeasurably superior to *Two-Way Family Favourites*, although he would recall that he had to listen all the way through the *Grand Ole Opry* country show, broadcast live from Nashville, before he could begin to enjoy AFN's *American Chart Show*. This, he'd later evocatively recall, 'opened a skylight into a netherworld which was almost beyond your imagining'. Indeed, in today's world of round-the-clock media, MTV and satellite news, it's almost impossible to conceive of how remote US music and culture was to Brits in the 1950s.

In answer to Sue Lawley's polite probing on *Desert Island Discs*, John claimed to have neither liked nor loathed his time as a Salopian. 'I was sort of indifferent to it; it seemed inevitable. You're obliged to observe all sorts of ludicrous rules and privileges, and I'm always astonished, when I look back on it, that no one ever questioned any of this stuff, because now I don't think you could possibly get away with doing the things that were done then. When I try to describe it to my own children they think I'm making it up. And when you talk about it, it does sound like you're describing something that happened at least a hundred years ago.

'It was very brutal . . . I got beaten something like thirty times in my first term, and these were not for deliberate offences but just for having forgotten to do something; I was a rather forgetful chap. I was constantly in trouble.' He later revealed that his mother had recently given him his reports, which had been kept in a trunk in the attic: 'They were quite horrifying; I was appalled at just how ghastly I must have been – but it was just stupidity, not malevolent in any way at all.'

For the record, John Ravenscroft emerged with four General Certificate of Education passes at Ordinary level, one of which he disowns. 'My certificate credits me with Divinity, which I failed by a mile,' he smiled in one of his last interviews. 'I got it into my head that the examiners would be extremely bored by reading the same thing over and over again, so I wrote all my answers in what I considered to be the style of Damon Runyon. I got 11 per cent.' His perceptive housemaster did, indeed, remark on John's penchant for writing 'long and facetious essays'.

A musical footnote to John's earliest days at Shrewsbury came when he came across 'a chap who had a complete recording of the coronation of George VI. [The King] was a man I much admired, mainly because of the way he overcame his stammer and his shyness, and his speech in 1941, "A man stood at the gate of the year", I regard as one of the great recordings of all time.' This was how 'Zadok the Priest', which was played at George VI's coronation, came to be John's first *Desert Island Disc* nearly four decades later.

Incidentally, the former John Ravenscroft was not the only old Salopian to have made an impact on BBC Radio One. A certain Douglas Muggeridge had been recruited from the World Service ('head of the Chinese section,' sneered John later) in the late 1960s and appointed joint controller of Radios One and Two. Rather in the manner of a headmaster summoning errant pupils, he decided to have a series of tête-à-têtes with his new charges. John recalled that Muggeridge probably thought 'I would do something unpredictable and startling, like rub heroin into the roots of his hair'. Continuing with the story, he described how the radio controller was 'sitting at his enormous desk . . . At some point in the conversation I mentioned public schools and he brightened up a little at this idea . . . I said, "Actually, I went to one myself." He went, "Extraordinary! Which one?" He was assuming it was some minor public school somewhere on the south coast. I said, "Shrewsbury." At this stage, he was getting quite elated. "Which house were you in?" I told him and he asked, "How's Brookie?"

'It was clear that he thought, "Whatever he looks like, and whatever he plays on the radio, he is still 'one of us'." I think for a long time it was this factor that sustained me at the BBC.'

Having survived Shrewsbury, followed by six months spent working as an office boy for one of his father's competitors, John Ravenscroft's next adventure came with two years of compulsory National Service. This ritual was a hangover from wartime conscription, and was on the point of being abolished: indeed, by a cruel twist of fate, John found himself born a mere forty-eight hours too soon to avoid it. He served – as 23558538 Gunner Ravenscroft, J. – with the Royal Artillery, as a B2 Radar Operator at the Guided Weapons Trials Establishment on the island of Anglesey from the spring of 1957 to 1959. It was clearly a significant part of his life since, unlike his first marriage, it forms part of his entry in *Who's Who*: 'John Peel: see Ravenscroft, J. R. P.'!

As with his school experiences, John developed a coping mechanism for National Service that enabled him to swim, relatively undetected, below the surface and survive among people he would normally have run a mile to avoid – in this case, 'working-class squaddies from Clydebank' whose beatings he endured to earn grudging respect. He recalled, however, that his final report was altogether too reminiscent of those his parents had received from his educational alma mater: 'The Army said afterwards, "At no time has he shown any sign of adapting to the military way of life." I took it as a compliment.'

John's spell in uniform also saw him serve as an unlikely goalkeeper in the company's hockey team. And he was perversely proud to be the only public schoolboy in his regiment not to be appointed an officer. As with his relative failure at school, there was a streak of rebellion apparent here, because this was also the time at which he first became conscious of the sound of his voice: 'A public-school accent got you into an awful lot of trouble, so I tried to flatten it.'

To complicate matters still further, while John was in basic training, his commanding officer happened to be going out with his stepsister (his parents having divorced when he was about sixteen and settled down in new circumstances): 'He was enough of a prick that when I met him at home I was obliged to call him "sir",' he fumed in later life. 'I've often hoped that one of these days I'll find him in flames at the side of the road, begging me to piss on it to put it out, and I shall say, "No, no. You carry on," and pass by on the other side.'

Money was understandably in short supply – 'I was only on 25 bob [£1.25] a week,' he'd later grumble – so he found a cost-effective way to sate his appetite for music by buying his records via a dealer in Holland. Discs sent directly from the United States attracted a prohibitive amount of duty, so this Dutch importer provided a useful service to folk, jazz and blues buffs by sending them their listening from closer at hand. When in London, Peel would also visit Dobells, a famous record shop centrally situated in Charing Cross Road which was famous for its eclectic stock.

On his re-emergence from National Service after twenty-four months, he found his first proper stop on civvy street working for his father's business, which was followed closely by a spell in Rochdale as a mill operator from 1959–60. Although relations with his father remained distant, when he offered young John a paid passage to the United States – the pretext being that he could learn the cotton trade at first hand there – he was quick to take him up on it. 'My dad asked me what I was going to do,' he recalled in a *Record Collector* interview, 'and I said "Sit around a while, probably." My father said, "Will you go to America if I send you?" So I thought I'd call his bluff!'

2

Adventures in America

IN SPRING 1960, after accepting his father's offer of a paid-for voyage to the States, the twenty-year-old John Ravenscroft found himself on board the SS *Eugene Lykes*, en route for Houston (air travel was, at this pre-jumbo jet stage, still the preserve of the mega-rich). The journey was a balmy one, and John spent much of it spreadeagled face-up on deck enjoying the spectacular mid-Atlantic sunsets. His arrival at Houston, however, soon dispelled all such memories – on his first night in the Texan city he witnessed a fatal stabbing. Swiftly hopping on a train to nearby Dallas, he spent his first night in the local YMCA 'before making a quick exit after being accosted by a rather hot-blooded male'. Shades of Shrewsbury . . .

Seemingly set on a coals-to-Newcastle adventure, the eager young man had packed a selection of rare blues records in his hand-luggage, which, in effect, he was bringing to the very home of the blues. He'd prepared for his trip before he left Britain by catching legendary rock'n'rollers Eddie Cochran and Gene Vincent at the Liverpool Empire in April 1960, just days before a car crash took Cochran's life and left Vincent with a disfiguring limp. Interestingly, one man involved with the organization of that tour was John's future manager and confederate Clive Selwood, then making the transition from small-time singer to music-business mogul. Of equal note is the fact that both men separately highlighted the point at which Cochran swivelled 180 degrees to face his audience, singing the first line of Ray Charles's 'Hallelujah I Love Her So', as one of the most exciting moments in all their years of witnessing rock shows.

So it was that John Ravenscroft set foot in the land of opportunity in 1960, little realizing that three years later, the music emerging from of his native Merseyside would, by association, make him something of a celebrity. The Beatles played their first lunchtime gig at the sweaty Cavern Club in Liverpool in early 1961, and within a couple of years their every move was being reported to the waiting world by television and radio. In the States at least, any 'expert' opinion from someone who had grown up in the very city that had spawned the Fab Four would be worth its weight in gold.

Dallas proved to be a congenial city for the young Englishman. Having started work as a computer programmer for an insurance company on Central Expressway, he enjoyed a memorable brush with history in November 1963 by attending a press conference after President John F. Kennedy was assassinated. (This took place a few days before chief suspect Lee Harvey Oswald was shot and killed by local strip-club owner Jack Ruby.) After the announcement of Kennedy's assassination, John had driven into town and had been astounded to find he could breach the police cordon around the scene of the crime simply by claiming to be a correspondent from the *Liverpool Echo*.

After three-quarters of an hour spent observing proceedings, he attempted to right his wrong by calling the *Echo* to give them his story, but the response he received from the newspaper's office was decidedly unenthusiastic: 'I was a bit wounded by that, but then that night a mate and I were driving around and there was nothing to do, so I figured we'd go down to police headquarters and see what's going on. We went down there and I asked the police officer what's happening. He said, "There's a press conference in a few minutes," pointing to a flight of steps at the edge of the building.'

Reclaiming his *Liverpool Echo* persona and press-ganging his friend Bob into being his photographer – 'although we didn't have a pen or paper or camera between us' – they witnessed the identification parade in the basement at which alleged assassin Oswald was introduced. Indeed, film of the press conference exists that shows John and Bob standing in the background, 'looking like tourists', in John's words.

The previous year had brought an unexpected but welcome introduction to the media for John when he fronted up at local Dallas radio station WRR with some of the blues records he'd brought with him from home. One of his most prized purchases from Dobells had been *Rooster Crowed In England* by Lightnin' Hopkins, and he would later claim that this had been his passport to the airwaves. Surprisingly, until the likes of the Rolling Stones, Yardbirds and Animals reintroduced the United States to its long-lost blues heritage, it was almost impossible to get hold of authentic recordings by the masters in their native country. Labels such as Bluebird in France, with their 'race' catalogue, were leading the way. However, John was startled to find he knew more about the music than those hosting *Kat's Karavan*, the rhythm-and-blues show on which he appeared.

The other thing that shocked him was hearing his voice, which thanks to his expensive education and despite his National Service efforts, was still reminiscent, in his own words, of 'a minor member of the royal family. Amazingly high-pitched, too . . .' It certainly contrasted with the deep, evocative tones of the two hosts with whom he worked. It would not be long before John would cut his ties conclusively with his public-school past and begin to modify his speaking voice, both in timbre and accent, to reflect his regional origins. 'When the Beatles came along,' he once reminisced, 'the Americans needed someone with something that resembled a Liverpool accent. So I obliged.' This would surely have horrified his father who had, after all, paid many hundreds of pounds to put his first-born through the 'system', but it had to be done. Hooray Henrys from Heswall and Merseyside moptops most certainly didn't belong together.

At this stage, John's DJ work was certainly not sufficient for him to give up his day job: 'It was ten-to-midnight, as far as I can remember. I just did one night a week, Monday nights, a kind of half a programme. It only lasted a few weeks and then I asked – at least suggested – that they started paying me, and they told me to bugger off.' He was clearly already in training for the nocturnal broadcasting slots with which he'd become associated, for in order to further his music career, John began to frequent a bowling alley, the grandly named Cotton Bowling Palace, from where KLIF broadcast an all-night show that started at midnight. His tactic of coming home from work and catnapping before heading off to the bowling alley failed to bear fruit initially, but when the station's star presenter Russ Knight (aka 'the Weird Beard') started 'talking a load of codswallop about Liverpool when the Beatles came over', John saw his chance and seized it with both hands. It helped, he later recalled, that 'Americans had this idea that if you lived in the UK there were probably only a couple of hundred people and they were bound to know each other.'

Knight was so won over by Dallas's very own Merseybeat expert that he sent him to a downtown department store to hand out free Beatles albums as a publicity stunt. John survived his first mobbing by members of the opposite sex, and decided he liked the experience. The die was cast: he was a Beatles expert, despite never having met the group. Unfortunately, his attempts to reach them on their first visit to Dallas in September 1964 were unsuccessful, but he would nevertheless field phone calls from listeners eager to find out if he knew the colour of Paul's eyes. These were generally answered 'after the next record', which at least gave him the chance to consult some reference books.

By the time the Beatles came along John had been living in Dallas for four years, 'working principally as an office boy, which I thoroughly enjoyed. But it was one of those things where my father would write me anguished letters saying, "How are you getting on in your career?" and I'd say, "Well, I'm still an office boy with every prospect of remaining one."' Life was clearly changing for the better, though, and the Republic National Life Insurance Company would soon be a part of his past.

Like many ex-public schoolboys, the young John Ravenscroft had found relating to the opposite sex an excruciatingly difficult proposition. Single-sex schools, not to mention the homosexual practices they frequently gave rise to, hardly turned out young men ready to enter fulfilling relationships. Indeed, so backward had John been in coming forward that his father had been convinced he was gay. 'I'd pay five pounds if you came home and told me you'd got a barmaid pregnant,' was Ravenscroft Sr's most memorable offering on the subject. But Dallas was to inspire the young man, barely out of his teens and still mired in adolescent angst, to lose his inhibitions – and plenty more besides.

At this point, John lived in a converted shed 'at the bottom of somebody's garden, which had been slave quarters in a previous century'. And this is where the girls who 'wanted to snog someone from England' came. But virginity was still regarded as something to be retained for one's wedding night – which meant, John later reflected, that 'They'd do anything except shag you.' His first girlfriend was a redhead, Judy Garrison, who was no underage would-be Beatles groupie, but many of his Dallas conquests were somewhat younger.

In 1996, Q magazine went digging for scandal, and found some. In an interview titled 'Who The Hell Does John Peel Think He Is?' (the 'Who The Hell . . .' series revolved around a deliberately provocative question-and-answer session), journalist Adrian Deevoy brought up the subject of John having been held at gunpoint by an enraged Texan in 1965, who allegedly suspected the DJ of having had sexual relations with his thirteen-year-old daughter. Deevoy may well have been surprised at the straight answer his question received. 'Despite my appearance now as the bloke who has come to collect the empties, there was once a time when I was really rather gorgeous,' John revealed. 'And somebody used to come round fairly regularly for my clumsy services who turned out to be rather younger than I'd imagined.'

The upshot of this was that John was almost shot. Taking the object of his affection home, he found himself with a gun to his head, her father having waited in a ditch for their arrival. An interrogation at gunpoint with 'an armed, angry father who thinks you've been shagging his daughter' resulted, which rendered young Ravenscroft 'about as frightened as it's possible to get'.

Whether or not this encounter had a bearing on John's

decision to settle down later that same year is uncertain. We do know that 1965 saw him meet and marry his first wife, Shirley Anne Milburn. It was almost a month after his twenty-sixth birthday – and she was only sixteen – when they married at the Christian Church of Durant in Oklahoma on 26 September. However, their union would not be a happy one. Understandably, Peel was never keen to talk about it and, when pressed by *Q*'s Deevoy, in the writer's words, 'An unusual and difficult silence descended.'

There has always been controversy about Shirley's age – not least that the couple married in Oklahoma, where the legal age for such ceremonies was sixteen, while in Texas, where her family lived, the legal age of consent was seventeen. Peel himself told Deevoy she was fifteen, which was legal 'in that particular state'. However, he excused himself from further questioning on the grounds that Shirley was dead. Although she would later cross the Atlantic with him, the relationship was to break down completely by 1969 and the couple divorced in 1971. Even so, she stayed in Britain for most of the rest of her short and tragic life.

Ironically, her father, Jesse Milburn, had run a school for would-be radio and TV announcers until the business foundered, but he had died in a car crash the same year his daughter married John, her mother also dying within the month. Before those crushing blows, the Milburn family had, according to elder sister Yvette, been as strait-laced and distant as the Ravenscrofts appeared to be: 'We had quiet, good parents, but emotionally they were like strangers to us. Our mother encouraged the relationship [with John]; I didn't approve because he was so much older than her, but he was British and mother thought from his accent that he was from the upper class. And she thought he would be a rock for her to cling on to.'

When John Peel broke his silence over the marriage in 1969, he put its failure down to the fact that, 'We had differing ideals which perhaps weren't right.' Later, he'd liken the union to a mutual defence pact: 'I'm sure I wasn't blameless. She was just as fucked-up as any fifteen-year-old who'd just lost her parents would be, and married some geezer from another planet.'

Certainly, none of his companions seemed to have much to say in her favour. Clive Selwood's memoirs recall Shirley flinging a red-hot iron at her husband when they were living in a tiny flat in London's King's Road, pursuing him 'down the road and around the block, both barefoot, with John trying to offer explanations over his shoulder and Shirley, in the absence of more flat irons, hurling abuse'.

Trevor Dann, Peel's superior at Radio One in the 1990s, recalls hearing tales about how she had physically beaten him up, often waiting until he was asleep before commencing her assaults. Whatever the truth, it was an episode in John Peel's life that he would live to regret, not least when Shirley, on her third marriage and having become dependent on alcohol and prescription drugs, choked on a chicken bone and was found dead in her own vomit in 1987.

Back in 1965, John Ravenscroft was finally on the up. Having won over the residents of Dallas with his Merseybeat mastery, John found himself on the second rung of the career ladder when he applied for and was successful in securing his first full-time post at radio station KOMA in Oklahoma City. Here he finally got to meet the Beatles when they held a press conference in nearby Minneapolis. The history books appear to date this as 21 August 1965, the sixth stop on their second full US tour. On the journey to Minneapolis John was accompanied by a fellow Liverpudlian, whose brother was a drummer with minor-league Merseybeaters the Escorts.

Unfortunately, so keen was John's companion to establish kinship with the Beatles that the array of questions he lobbed at the band (one such example being, 'Would you fancy a pan of Scouse?') not surprisingly saw him receive the sharp end of Lennon's tongue.

Flustered by this distraction, John (Ravenscroft, not Lennon) failed to hit his interviewing stride – something that would, sometimes embarrassingly, prove a recurring problem during his later career. In fact, so disappointed was he with his performance that he didn't even wait to listen to his recording but ripped the tape reel from the machine (not forgetting that this was long before the days of cassette recorders or Dictaphones) and threw it into a waste bin at the Twin Cities' Metropolitan Stadium where the band were to play that night. ('I wish I still had it,' he'd later lament.) An altogether disappointing day was further spoiled by an altercation with an over-zealous security guard, who pushed our man down some stairs, the upshot being that his sole memory of the concert itself was Lennon pretending to use his guitar as a baseball bat as he crossed the diamond.

More happily, John's spell in the Midwest saw him develop a radio double act with Paul Miller, the first of several he'd enjoy over the course of his career (the others included Peel and Drummond, Peel and Walters, and Peel and Jensen). The imaginatively titled *Paul and John Show*, a breakfast-time broadcast, was the result. The music was fairly standard chart fare, with little scope for John to influence the playlist: the emphasis was more on what was said between records.

'It was an American Top Forty station that wanted a British DJ,' he later reflected. 'Back then, there was all sorts of Canadian DJs, many of them calling themselves James Bond. Almost every station had a Canadian who pretended to be called James Bond, because apparently to an American ear they can't tell the difference between an English accent and a Canadian accent. That seems extraordinary to me, but this is what they used to claim. You'd be driving around in somewhere like Kansas and you'd switch on a local radio station and there'd be a guy on there going, "Hi there, I'm James Bond, I'm Ringo Starr's cousin!" Come on, do me a favour! Anyway, I was at KOMA for a year, being their kind of British expert.'

The DJ underwent a subtle name-change around this time too. 'When I started working full-time at KOMA, I was known as John Ravencroft, when in fact my real name is John Ravenscroft, with an "s" in the middle of it,' he later explained. 'But the Americans apparently believed that "Ravenscroft" was too much for any one person to remember.'

In time, John Ravencroft – described in a promotional poster as 'He's English! He's What's Happening, Baby! He's On KOMA . . . Naturally' – began to find himself live work outside the confines of the station, something that would prove to be a recurring feature of his career. Clive Selwood, in his entertaining memoirs, recalled John telling him about one gig that he played at an Indian reservation: 'On this occasion, the heady combination of music and hard liquor resulted in [him sustaining] a heavy beating from a group of Native Americans. On the next reservation appearance he hired a couple of braves as bodyguards and watched in dismay as, fuelled by liquor, the two of them set about everyone else!'

John also diversified into managing a couple of local groups. Both rejoiced in names redolent of the times – one being Dann Yankee and the Carpetbaggers, the other Jay Walker and the Pedestrians. He'd later recall to *Record Collector*'s Mark Paytress that the local venues had a depressingly conservative musical policy at the time: 'They'd say to you, "Do they play 'Hang On Sloopy' and 'Louie

Louie'?" and if you could say "Yes" they'd say, "We'll book 'em." That's all they wanted to know. And then you'd get paid and drive back home.'

It was around this time that Peel's love affair with the automobile took off in earnest – a relationship he freely admitted was at odds with the ecologically friendly vegetarian he was to become: 'The first car I bought for myself was a 1958 Chevrolet Biscayne, and then I had a 1961 model. But I drove that from Friendly Chevy in Dallas straight into the side of a truck.' In the future he would remain accident-free – surprisingly so, given some of the cars he drove: 'I had a 1963 Chevy Impala, and then the 409 cubic-inch Super Sports model. That was insanely powerful – most of them just blew up.' Later he had an ultra-desirable 1963 Corvette, and he kept another 1963 Impala.

John's straight-man act on the airwaves to Paul Miller's comic capers proved reasonably popular, but things eventually changed. 'After a while they moved me to the evening with a bloke called Davis, who always referred to himself as a "Josh Dickie" – and I remember thinking I wasn't very keen on the concept of "josh dickies". Nice lad, though!' The teaming-up with Oklahoma's answer to Dave Lee Travis failed to spark, however, and John and KOMA parted company after some eighteen months.

Undeterred, John applied for two more jobs in radio – one in San Diego and the other at radio station KMEN in San Bernardino. He chose the latter not because it was in sunny California, where the Beach Boys ruled the waves and airwaves, but simply because the name appealed to him: 'That was the only reason, the money was the same.' And so his move to the West Coast in 1965 duly signalled the start of an extraordinary new chapter in the broadcasting career of the fledgling josh dickie from England.

3

California Dreams
and Piracy

BY THE TIME John Raven(s)croft reached southern California, cultural change was in the air. Bob Dylan was at his peak of his powers, while the Byrds, darlings of the burgeoning longhair scene in Los Angeles, had set the charts on fire across the world with their chiming, pungent, electric folk-rock. Singles such as their version of 'Mr Tambourine Man' and the legendary 'Eight Miles High' had shown that America wasn't taking the British invasion lying down, and Sunset Strip rocked to the sound of McGuinn, Crosby and company, not to mention fellow West Coasters such as Love, the Doors and Buffalo Springfield.

Further north, the original US Charlatans had taken possession of the Red Dog Saloon in the tiny Nevada town of Virginia City and turned themselves into the original acid-rock band, crystallizing a style of druggie folk and blues music that would become universally recognized two years later as the San Francisco Sound. In the audience at the Red

Dog were members of Jefferson Airplane, the Grateful Dead, Quicksilver Messenger Service and Big Brother and the Holding Company, all of whom would take this template and use it to become big stars of psychedelic rock.

John was in the right place at the right time once again, and well aware that something special was happening on the West Coast – 'You couldn't help but feel it.' And though his second-hand Beatles connections were now wearing thin, he was ideally placed to tap into the new counter-culture growing in peaceful opposition to the increasing American involvement in the Vietnam War. Music was one of their most potent means of protest against Kennedy's successor President Johnson and the powers that be.

The tribes were gathering. The youth of southern California was finding escape in love-ins in Griffith Park and in the wonders of drugs such as marijuana and LSD (lysergic acid diethylamide), a psychedelic stimulant espoused by such high priests as academic Timothy Leary and novelist Ken Kesey and his Merry Pranksters. The latter held 'acid tests' up and down the Pacific Coast, during which they would hand out 'trips' of LSD in liquid form.

San Bernardino is a quiet town some sixty miles east of LA, and it was here that John found himself in early 1966 after losing his job at KOMA in Oklahoma City: 'Since I was the last guy they'd taken on, I was the first they got rid of when the going got rough. So I . . . went off to work in California, where I started taking drugs and leading a generally depraved sort of life.'

Now on the staff of radio station KMEN, the DJ soon found himself hanging around with a band called the Mystics, part of a mainly blues-based local scene that also included Bush and the North Side Moss. He regularly went to local shows and even experienced an early performance by the Seeds, led by legendary cult figure Sky Saxon whom he recalled as 'very, very freaky and interesting for the time'.

One day he went down to a show that the Mystics and the Moss were putting on in a shopping mall in nearby Riverside. As he'd later recall in *ZigZag* magazine: 'The Mystics did their set, but before the North Side Moss were due to go on, there was this band that nobody had heard of who had also been booked. I was planning to go and have a wander around the shopping centre while they were playing, but as I was about to drift off I saw them taking the stage and starting to tune up. They looked very weird and freaky so I decided to hang around to see if they were any good. They called themselves, it transpired, the Misunderstood. Well, it was like one of your St Paul on the road to Damascus experiences – it was stunning! Riveting! They cut both the North Side Moss and the Mystics to pieces.'

The quintet were obviously fans of both the Yardbirds and the Paul Butterfield Blues Band, whose seminal second album *East West* had just been released. Ostensibly a blues band doing Howlin' Wolf-type material, the Misunderstood were beginning to progress to something far more exciting to John's ears – steel guitarist Glenn Ross Campbell wailed like a banshee, bassist Steve Whiting played his bass with a bottleneck, and they would radically rearrange old standards such as 'Shake Your Money Maker' into wild rave-ups, giving them their own unique edge. They were also among the very first group, if not *the* first, to experiment with guitar feedback – an effect the Who would later make their own. The Misunderstood became the first of many groups that John would mentor and give encouragement to – he even financed an LP's worth of music, recorded at Phil Spector's Gold Star Studio in Hollywood, which was intended as a demo to secure a record deal.

It was quite an idyllic time for both the band and their English Svengali, as John later recalled: 'They used to do the odd gig, but most of the time we'd just sit around and talk about the possibilities of the future. They were so good compared with any other band I'd heard 'til then – much better and certainly more inventive – and this, don't forget, was at a time when you could drive in to Los Angeles and see the Byrds or Love almost any time you wanted.' He'd also been present at some of the recording sessions that produced Jefferson Airplane's legendary debut album *Surrealistic Pillow*, which contained the infamous drug anthem 'White Rabbit'. Not that John overindulged in a wide range of mood-enhancing substances: 'We used to sit around and smoke a lot, but it wasn't in any way sinister. We had these mates who would go into LA every so often and literally cram the boot of their car full of grass.'

The Misunderstood might have been trying to push the boundaries of rock, but they rarely played live. John recalled one extra-special show in particular that was 'the most incredible gig I ever saw them do. It was at a club called Pandora's Box, which was subsequently closed down – the act that sparked the Sunset Strip riots about which Buffalo Springfield sang "For What It's Worth". The predominant feel in LA at that time was the ultra-cool thing. I'd met the Byrds a while earlier and none of them had so much as spoken! I was compering a gig of theirs and went in to say hello, but they just stood there and didn't say a word. What a bunch of twats, I thought. But that was the basic attitude you had to adopt in Los Angeles.

'So when the Misunderstood went down there to play Pandora's Box, they were the subject of much ridicule simply because they were from Riverside, which was approximately the equivalent to coming from, say, Stowmarket in England.

There was a lot of ho, ho, ho, a band from Riverside, they'll be a bunch of hicks, ho, ho, ho – that sort of thing. Anyway, the first band went on and they were fairly ordinary, and then the Misunderstood went on. It was just like one of those silly scenes from a Cliff Richard film where everybody in the place gradually stopped talking and drifted towards the stage – even the bar closed temporarily because the barman wanted to watch! They used to do this thing where they'd get a cyclical feedback noise repeating every few seconds – they'd leave the stage with their instruments feeding back and then go back on again a minute or so later. That sort of thing became commonplace a few years later, of course, but in mid-'66 it just freaked everybody out completely. When they finished their set there was just total silence; people had never seen anything like it in their lives.'

Yet despite the occasional such humdinger, the group seemed to be getting nowhere fast and, in June 1966 Ravenscroft suggested that they should go to London and try to make it there. Four members of the band – Campbell, Whiting, guitarist Greg Treadway and drummer Rick Moe – duly took a boat; singer Rick Brown was delayed because of a run-in with the military draft. With hotels beyond their limited budget, John gave them his mother's address – now divorced, she had a flat in London's Notting Hill. Unfortunately, she hadn't been told they were coming (transatlantic phone calls in those days were major events) and the Misunderstood were forced to sit out on the street for hours awaiting her return.

Eventually, through contacts of John's youngest brother Alan, the group signed a contract with Fontana Records, releasing just one 7-inch single in early 1967. 'I Can Take You To The Sun', with English guitarist Tony Hill replacing Treadway, was far more musically adventurous than the blues-based fare they'd been playing in Riverside, and made a huge impact on the British music scene of the time. It perfectly encapsulated everything that was unique about the era, within the confines of a swirling, three-minute rock song, with mysterious lyrics, distortion, feedback and acoustic interludes. Beautifully sung by Rick Brown, it remains one of the great psychedelic singles of all time, and was a record the young DJ would air a great deal upon his eventual return to the UK.

Sadly, the Misunderstood never got a proper chance to develop this exciting new direction, as Uncle Sam finally caught up with their singer. 'Rick was drafted into the army,' John recalled, 'but then a strange situation developed: he returned to California and we got hold of a crooked psychiatrist up in San Francisco, to whom we sent Rick with about $300 in search of a certificate declaring him unfit for military service. But that didn't work for one reason and another, and he was sent off for army training prior to being shipped off to Vietnam, presumably. Within weeks he'd deserted and ended up in India! The Misunderstood could've been astonishingly influential – Rick wasn't the central figure, but without him they were headless and just seemed to break up in disorder. They tried to replace him, but no one else would have been able to fill his place. He was the one who continually led them into new ideas and things.'

By this time, John was about to leave America himself under what he'd refer to as a 'slight cloud'. The local sheriff's department had had a long-running conflict with KMEN, and was investigating various radio-station employees for alleged misdemeanours. According to the DJ the sheriff was 'determined to close the station down', with the result that John himself became a target. He booked a flight under his two middle names of Robert Parker, fled the long arm of the law and made it safely back to the land of his birth. But as he was soon to discover, the England that he'd left in 1960 was a very different place to the one he returned to early in 1967.

In the wake of the enormous public appetite for pop music spearheaded by the likes of the Beatles and the Rolling Stones, there had been a corresponding revolution in broadcasting. The year 1964 had witnessed the arrival of pirate radio, which was based on a format similar to that used in America and set up in direct competition to the UK state radio controlled by the BBC. The pirates fulfilled a demand from a quickly expanding teenage population frustrated by the BBC Light Programme's failure to cater for a round-the-clock pop audience. The BBC found it difficult to play as many pop records as teenagers would have liked since, tied to the Musicians' Union apron strings, they had to play a fixed proportion of live music in order to ensure that performing musicians could make a living. This was the so-called 'needle time' restriction, referring to stylus-on-vinyl time.

Prior to the pirates, the teen audience had got much of their popular music on Radio Luxembourg, but it was only possible to listen to that at night. Only at weekends did the BBC play more than a couple of hours of the latest sounds. The rest of time they had to feature dance bands more familiar with the sounds of the 1940s than the sounds of the 1960s. The pirates played the latest pop round the clock, gaining income from heavy amounts of advertising, and circumventing prosecution from the government by broadcasting from ships moored around the coastline of the UK. Former record-plugger Ronan O'Rahilly founded Radio Caroline, which broadcast from two locations as Caroline North and South. The other key player was Radio London.

'Big L', as it was known, had been set up by a consortium of Texas businessmen headed by Don Pierson and Tom Dannaher, who thought they could go one better than

Caroline. Radio London was on the air by December 1964, broadcasting from an ex-Second World War minesweeper re-christened the MV *Galaxy*, which was fitted with a powerful 50-kilowatt transmitter requiring an aerial mast taller than Nelson's Column. The boat was moored three-and-a-half miles off Frinton-on-Sea in Essex, and soon had a large audience hooked on the novelty of its American-style jingles (later immortalized on the Who's *Sell Out* LP) and the sheer quality of the programming.

For a long time, Big L and its fellow pirates seemingly got away with murder, blithely ignoring the Performing Rights Society, which was supposed to earn a royalty from every record played on air. Its playlists were heavily interspersed with corporate advertising by a clientele that included Coca-Cola, Heinz and the *News of the World*. But this didn't appear to bother the station's young audience.

On his return from the States with first wife Shirley, John had settled into what was now being referred to as 'Swinging London', the new music and fashion capital of the world, but found it difficult to get work at first. An introduction from his next-door neighbour, who advertised on the station, led to a job on Big L. Joining the station in March 1967, he quickly secured the graveyard shift of midnight to 2 a.m. – two weeks on the boat and one off, the latter being spent on shore leave in England – and made it his own. Working for an illegal pirate radio station, it was necessary to use a false name for broadcasting purposes to protect his true identity, and so, at the suggestion of a secretary who observed that Ravenscroft was a bit of a mouthful, he adopted the Peel moniker. He named his show *The Perfumed Garden*, taking its title from a notorious book of the same name – an erotic volume like the *Kama Sutra* – which fitted in perfectly with the spirit of the times.

Peel's influence appeared on the occasional daytime show too. Big L DJs were asked to select a 'Climber of the Week', which was added to the Top Forty playlist – among those that Peel backed were Denny Laine's 'Say You Don't Mind', Peanut Butter Conspiracy's 'It's A Happening Thing' and 'Omaha' by Moby Grape.

Pirate broadcasting wasn't the only phenomenon that was sweeping the UK. The peace and love message that had taken root on the US West Coast while Peel was there was beginning to be heard in Europe. The baby boomers were waking up and deciding that there was more to life than the grim nine-to-five straitjacket existence led by their fathers, who'd fought in the Second World War. The very black-and-white Macmillan era of the 1950s was about to turn Day-Glo!

By 1967 and the so-called Summer of Love, the counter-culture – or 'underground' as it was also known – was making its mark through experiments in alternative lifestyles, environmentalism, the sexual revolution and, eventually, women's liberation. For many 'weekend hippies', though, the alternative society began and ended with recreational drugs and the amazing musical soundtrack that was one of the era's greatest cultural contributions. The advent of the rock revolution, as exemplified by the Beatles' *Sgt Pepper's Lonely Hearts Club Band*, was so complete that it dominated art at the expense of film, painting and literature.

It was during his time on board the MV *Galaxy* that Peel set out his musical stall. He'd later observe: 'You need a programme where the people who are listening are not treated as though they are totally moronic.' Ignoring the Top Forty playlists of fellow DJs such as Ed Stewart and Kenny Everett, he chose to highlight records by artists as obscure as Captain Beefheart, John Fahey, Country Joe and the Fish, Jefferson Airplane and Lightnin' Hopkins, and would give over whole segments of the show to airing masterworks such as the just-released *Sgt Pepper* and the lesser-known but achingly hip Incredible String Band's *The 5,000 Spirits Or The Layers Of The Onion*. Much of this music was not readily available in local record stores, not yet anyway, but it was magnificently different to the mainstream, and many young ears and minds were opened as a result of hearing it.

Less impressively in retrospect, perhaps, Peel would also read out poetry, as well as articles from the new underground press, including magazines such as *Oz* and *International Times*, and talk about political issues. His biggest asset, however, was his human touch. He fostered a kind of intimacy with his growing band of listeners that made them feel he was talking and playing music for them and them alone. It was out on the ocean wave that he began to adopt his quietly spoken, self-effacing delivery, which was in marked contrast to the histrionics of his fellow jocks. Peel and the new music found their way into countless hearts.

He also encouraged correspondence. As he'd later tell the *Listener* magazine: 'You had a remarkable two-way dialogue with the audience which is not possible to simulate on land. You put the show out completely on your own in the bowels of a rotten ship three miles out at sea. You knew the audience felt a little bit daring even listening to you.'

One of those listeners was a young musician from Wimbledon called Mark Feld. Feld had been a face on the London Mod scene since the early 1960s and, being heavily into fashion, had also been the subject of a feature by *Town* magazine. He'd released a couple of singles and, by early 1967, had become part of John's Children, a Mod-psychedelic band with attitude whose single 'Desdemona' had been banned by the Beeb for containing the risqué line, 'lift up your skirt and speak'. Mark had allegedly also spent time with a real-life wizard in France and was one of a number of Mods who'd opted for the hippie lifestyle. He sent Peel a copy of his single 'Hippie Gumbo', which the DJ duly played on his programme, and a close friendship soon developed between the two of them which would continue into the early 1970s.

Peel's life was soon to undergo a further dramatic shift, however. Radio London was living on borrowed time: the Labour government, tired of being made to look weak and inept by the pirates, took measures to silence them once and for all with the introduction of the draconian Marine Broadcasting Act. This came into force at midnight on 14 August 1967, its architect the Minister of Technology Tony Benn, and at a stroke rendered pirate radio illegal. While the government may or may not have had a point in saying that the stations' signals interrupted the communications of shipping in the North Sea and the emergency services on land, it was obvious that the real motive was economic: the state wanted to regain control of broadcasting.

For many, it was the end of an era. Big L shut at 3 p.m. on the 14th after a final hour of tributes from the likes of Mick Jagger and Ringo Starr, and its DJs were mobbed when they arrived at London's Liverpool Street station. In one final V-sign to authority, the last record played was 'A Day In The Life' from the *Sgt Pepper* LP – a track the BBC had banned due to its drug references.

As the government fired its final cannonball across the bows of the pirate ships, the BBC was already drawing up radical plans to reorganize its broadcasting policy. After all, the government couldn't afford to alienate thousands of potential Labour voters. It announced the formation of four rejuvenated services – Radios One, Two, Three and Four, of which Radio One would go some way towards replacing the

Radio listeners enjoyed John Peel's deadpan delivery for almost forty years, from his early days broadcasting on the pirate radio station Radio London (its 'offices' *below*), to his pioneering years with the BBC.

Right: Collecting one of his many industry honours, Peel triumphantly claims the *Melody Maker* music award for Best Disc Jockey in 1969.

Below: With Eric Clapton at the same awards ceremony.

Above: The original line-up of Radio One DJs, pictured here at the launch of the then-ground-breaking station in 1967. John was involved from the beginning (*front row, far right*).

Below: Thirty years later, the reunion photoshoot.

Larking about at the Reading Festival *circa* 1970 (*left*) and chatting with Elton John at the same festival in 1977 (*below*).

With Damon Albarn at the 1996 Phoenix Festival (*above*).

The appeal of the music fests never faded with time – John was still soaking up the Glastonbury atmosphere in 2003 (*right*).

Left: John enjoyed a thirty-year marriage with his wife, Sheila, whom he affectionately referred to as 'the Pig', on account of her snorting laugh. They wed on 31 August 1974.

Right: Proud dad John with Sheila and their newborn son William, in 1976. William was the first of John's four children, all of whom he frequently mentioned on air.

John's time at home and with family was hugely important to him. He is seen here with the family dog in 1973 (*right*) and at home in 'Peel Acres' in 1990 (*below*), with just a fraction of his extensive record collection on display. Many of Peel's shows were actually broadcast from home, and his living room was host to a number of impromptu live sessions.

A lifelong Liverpool FC fan, John was a dedicated visitor to Anfield (*below*) and was also known to take to the pitch himself – here shown at a charity football match in 1982 (*left*).

much-loved style of the pirates. Wisely, the powers that be decided that many of their new DJs would be the selfsame jocks who had lost their jobs when the pirates had been sunk.

It had been a long, strange trip for John Ravenscroft from southern California to the North Sea, and there was more strangeness to come.

4

Into Top Gear

WITH TYPICAL FORESIGHT, in early 1967 John Peel had already seen which way the wind was blowing and, ahead of the final shutdown of Radio London, had begun to make overtures to the BBC about transplanting both himself and his *Perfumed Garden* to the corridors of Broadcasting House.

Peel had written to Mark White, deputy head of the BBC's Radio Gramophone Department, in late July 1967, enclosing a tape of his show and expressing the hope that 'the pioneering work he'd been doing could transfer to the BBC'. Nothing came of this request, but fortunately there was a producer in the organization who had already taken considerable notice of the DJ.

Bernie Andrews had joined the Beeb at the age of twenty-four in 1957, at a time when rock'n'roll was huge in the USA but had barely been recognized by state radio in the UK. Over the next decade he would become as much a thorn in the corporation's side as his new protégé Peel would in the late 1960s. In the decade's early days, Andrews had been attached to pop programme *Saturday Club*, firstly as a tape operator and then eventually as a full-blown producer during a period when the BBC was starting to give more airtime to electric bands such as the Rolling Stones and the Beatles, the Animals, Manfred Mann and the Kinks. His recording techniques, booking policy and personal touch boosted the show's ratings and, as the onslaught of the Mersey Sound and beat boom became unstoppable, the Beeb asked Andrews to produce a brand-new show on the Light Programme.

The new programme was intended as a more progressive version of *Saturday Club* and, unlike its predecessor, would book rock bands from the word go. The first show was to be broadcast on 16 July 1964, but it still had no name. Andrews organized a competition through pop weekly *Disc & Music Echo*, which offered the prize of attending the recording of the first session – which just happened to be by the Fab Four at the absolute height of Beatlemania. So it was that *Top Gear* was born. Storming sessions by both the Beatles and Stones gave the new show immediate credibility, but it only lasted a year before the BBC axed it – and, despite the continuation of *Saturday Club* and *Easy Beat*, the Beeb rolled over and handed the reins of pop and rock broadcasting, temporarily at least, to the pirates.

Bernie sat in the wings and worked on a show called *Folk Room*, but remained in tune with the progress of the pirates and kept abreast of the best presenters. When the Beeb stepped into the breach and launched Radio One, *Top Gear* was given a second chance. The decision as to who would present it was left up in the air. Peel's name had been put forward, but the authorities at the BBC had vetoed the suggestion. New controller Robin Scott admired Peel but felt he was too much his own man to kowtow to a corporation.

Andrews knew it had to be Peel from the outset, but he cleverly played the game and, when *Top Gear* version two was launched between 2 p.m. and 5 p.m. on Sunday, 1 October 1967, it was jointly presented by former Radio London DJ Pete Drummond with Peel. However, it did feature many of the new acts the latter had already been pioneering, including Tomorrow, Traffic and Pink Floyd.

When the show's second edition was broadcast on the following Sunday, Peel was nowhere to be heard, though again the programme proved itself a forum for some of the best new and imaginative music being produced at that time. His absence was temporary, however, and there were sessions from Jeff Beck, the Kinks, Cream and singer-songwriter Roy Harper, whose music Peel would vociferously promote – despite the occasional hiccup in relations – for years to come. Interestingly, when the pair had a row on air some years later, Peel let slip his philosophy for surviving as a subversive in the employ of the government. When an obviously stoned Harper openly criticized the ruling Conservative government and the BBC during a live in-concert broadcast in 1971, a furious Peel responded in kind: 'If I might say a word in defence of the programme? I realize the BBC is a machine, but Roy Harper records for EMI, the largest recording organization in the world, and that's a machine too. Now, the important thing about machines is that you use them and don't let them use you!'

Although Peel began to gain some leverage on the bookings for *Top Gear*, hiring such acts as the Incredible String Band, Bernie Andrews's superiors were still very much anti-Peel. However, the visionary producer stuck to his guns and booked John for a further seven weeks, during which time he co-presented with Tommy Vance, a former DJ on Radios Caroline, London and Luxembourg.

This one act of commitment on Andrews's part not only paid off – audience research for the programme came up trumps in Peel's favour – but of course changed the face of rock music broadcasting for the next forty years. During that seven-week stint many artists that were destined to go on to bigger and better things played debut sessions – these included David Bowie, the Bonzo Dog Doo-Dah Band, Fleetwood Mac, Fairport Convention and Soft Machine. The programme on 18 December also featured Jimi Hendrix's final BBC session.

The broadcast on 4 February 1968 saw Peel finally enjoy total independence and solo billing, making *Top Gear* his very own for years to come. It came as no surprise that the show happened to feature the debut session by Captain Beefheart and his Magic Band, an artist whose name became synonymous with Peel's for successive generations of listeners. Born Don Van Vliet, Beefheart was a Californian musician who had spent his teenage years in the small desert town of Lancaster where he had met fellow avant-garde fan and pioneer Frank Zappa – then leading the Mothers of Invention (another Peel fave). The Captain's main influence in musical terms was Howlin' Wolf, but he'd turned his love of blues into something wholly unique. Experimenting with time signatures, contrapuntal rhythms and syncopation as well as psychedelic sound-effects, while writing some of the most unusual lyrics of the time, Beefheart was one of the more 'far-out' artists to gain Peel's blessing. There are listeners who claim their lives changed for ever when they heard the ear-numbing shriek of the theremin on 'Electricity', which John played regularly on Big L, from the Magic Band's debut LP *Safe As Milk*.

Beefheart became one of Peel's obsessions and, years later, he'd admit to the singer's biographer, Mike Barnes, that when he compèred their UK debut, he was moved to tears: 'I started to introduce them at Middle Earth [a fabled hippie club in London's Covent Garden], but was so overcome with emotion that I started crying and had to abandon my announcement halfway through. I said, "I never dreamed that I would have the opportunity to say these words to you – This is Captain Beefheart and his Magic Band!"'

In fact, the legendary Beefheart session recorded on 24 January in Maida Vale (where Peel sessions were carried out for years), nearly didn't happen at all because of a ruling from the Musicians' Union about reciprocal bookings – American singers could only do radio sessions if backed by English musicians. This almost derailed the good Captain, but the ever-resourceful Bernie persuaded the MU that, as the name implied, Beefheart was backed by a troupe of magicians. They were therefore allowed to perform . . . as a variety act!

When the Captain and his crew returned for more UK dates late in 1968, Peel offered his services as unpaid chauffeur, driving Don and drummer John 'Drumbo' French to live dates in a hired Mini. One of the dates was at a strange establishment in Kidderminster called Frank Freeman's Dancing School. On the way home, the Captain suddenly ordered Peel to stop the car because he wanted to listen to a tree! Peel, dumbfounded by the request, duly complied, but later admitted he was never certain he'd heard the command right in the first place – had the Captain actually said that he wanted a pee? On the night itself, Peel didn't get the chance to see exactly what Beefheart did – the eccentric singer simply got out of the car and disappeared into the night.

Regardless of such odd incidents, Peel maintained a friendship with Van Vliet that lasted right through to the end of his life – even beyond 1982, when the musician dropped the Beefheart moniker and quit the music business in favour of life as a painter in the Mojave Desert. However, even Peel could find the Captain a strange man to be friends with: 'You never really quite knew where you were with him. Even those of us who were really fond of him just found him utterly mystifying. His thought processes were just not the thought processes of anybody else that you were ever likely to meet. He was a classic lateral thinker.'

John was quick to promote acts he felt were worthy and, even before he had established himself as the true guiding light of *Top Gear*, had got his mate Marc Bolan (the aforementioned Mark Feld) a BBC session in the previous November. Marc had got together with percussionist Steve Took to form an acoustic duo called Tyrannosaurus Rex whose bluesy/folksy sound and pure buttercup-sandwich lyrics that would make even Donovan blush, had become a favourite at longhair haunts such as the UFO Club.

One of the group's most unusual characteristics was Bolan's Larry the Lamb-like singing style, which people either loved or hated. The sound obviously appealed to John, because among the other vocalists he championed were Roger Chapman of Family and, ten years later, Feargal Sharkey of the Undertones, both of whom had a similar 'bleating' quality to their vocals.

When Tyrannosaurus Rex auditioned for the BBC, the panel that hired the acts for sessions was split in its appraisal of the duo, one producer calling them 'Crap . . . and pretentious crap at that.' Needless to say, Marc and pals would have the last laugh, going on to become one of the biggest bands of the 1970s as the electrified (and abbreviated) T. Rex.

Back in 1968, their appearances were all very low key, with the duo often playing sets in discothèques as part of the grandly named *John Peel Roadshow*. Peel would tell the teenybopper audiences to shut up, then have the pair sit on the floor while they sang their songs full of Tolkien-esque images. The duo signed to Regal Zonophone Records and the first album, *My People Were Fair And Had Sky In Their Hair . . . But Now They're Content To Wear Stars On Their Brows*, was released in mid-1968. Produced by Tony Visconti, it not only featured a children's story read by Peel but also a short sleevenote by him, which seems to epitomize the spirit of the era: 'They rose out of the sad and scattered leaves of an older summer. During the hard grey winter they were tended and strengthened by those who love them. They blossomed with the coming of spring, children rejoiced and the earth sang with them. It will be a long and ecstatic summer.'

Peel stuck with Bolan through thick and thin, championing him at every turn, playing cuts from the group's second LP, *Prophets, Seers And Sages, The Angels Of The Ages*, and reading another story on the third Tyrannosaurus Rex LP, *Unicorn*. When Bolan split from Took and went electric on *Beard Of Stars*, Peel gave the new band more sessions and even went on the road with them, sitting cross-legged onstage and reading a short story or poem before Marc's main set. Yet the two men were eventually to fall out in a serious way.

There was no excuse for the cynical manner in which the 'boppin' elf', as he was nicknamed, dumped his friend in 1971 as he rode to the top of the British charts with the success of singles such as 'Hot Love' and 'Get It On'. Bolan dropped Peel like a hot brick, though the DJ later confessed that he was not entirely surprised: 'I was always aware. I wasn't so stupid that I didn't see that Marc had a harder side to his character than I was generally seeing. This never really came out until he became a star. He just moved on to other people, which, to me, was very upsetting, because I thought he was my best friend at the time. Then all of a sudden phone calls weren't returned; someone else would say, "Marc's really busy, he'll phone you later, man" and so on.'

This disappointment certainly informed Peel's future deliberately distant relationships with his musical heroes. But back in 1968 his friendship with Bolan was solid as a rock – the pair had even been flatmates for a time – and Peel must have been delighted to see this quirky duo make records and sign with former Pink Floyd managers Peter Jenner and Andrew King. Their agency, Blackhill Enterprises, would become one of the main bookers of underground bands during the next decade.

One of Jenner and King's lasting contributions to the late 1960s were the free concerts in Hyde Park. Modelling them on the many tribal gatherings in San Francisco's Golden Gate Park was fair enough, but persuading the authorities to let the biggest park in London host get-togethers of pot-smoking hippies was no small feat. A series of such events was to occur over the next few years, but for many, including Peel, the first on Saturday 29 June 1968 featuring Tyrannosaurus Rex, Roy Harper, Jethro Tull and Pink Floyd, was impossible to top.

John would later say: 'I always claim that the best outdoor event I've ever been to was the Pink Floyd concert in Hyde Park, when I hired a boat and rowed out and I lay in the bottom of the boat, in the middle of the Serpentine, and just listened to the band play. I think their music then suited the open air perfectly. It was – it sounds ludicrous now, it's the kind of thing you [could] get away with saying at the time and which now, in these harsher times, sounds a bit silly, but I mean it was like a religious experience, it was that marvellous. They played *A Saucerful Of Secrets* and things. They just seemed to fill the whole sky and everything. And to coincide perfectly with the lapping of the water and trees and everything. It just seemed the perfect event. I think it was the nicest concert I've ever been to.'

Pink Floyd were just one band whose name would be linked with Peel's over the years – but, as with the Captain and the boppin' elf, he maintained a long relationship with the Floyd, one that lasted well into the punk-rock era. In their early incarnation, the group were pretty much darlings of the British underground, having played two of the most significant events in its early evolution, the launch of *International Times* at London's Roundhouse in October 1966 and headlining the 14 Hour Technicolor Dream at Alexandra Palace the following April.

Peel's involvement was established early on, from playing early Floyd singles such as 'See Emily Play' on Big L, to the BBC session in late 1967 that demonstrated that all was not well with their original guiding light Syd Barrett. (The session saw the group lay down two legendary Barrett songs – 'Scream Thy Last Scream' and 'Vegetable Man' – both, in their way, perhaps indicative of an unsettled mind.) Then there was Peel's constant support during the years between the arrival of Dave Gilmour and the advent of mega-sellers such as *Dark Side Of The Moon*. Fans from that long-gone era will never forget broadcasts of songs such as 'Murderistic Woman' (better known as 'Careful With That Axe, Eugene') with its blood-curdling howls, and the peaceful rural ode to summer 'Grantchester Meadows'. Peel would often play whole albums by the group in one *Top Gear* programme.

He even managed to lure the elusive Syd Barrett into the studio for a magnificent session backed by Gilmour and Rick Wright in early 1970. As for the show at Mothers Club in Birmingham (where he regularly DJed between 1968 and 1970): 'I wrote such ecstatic reviews of it [specifically about 'Set The Controls For The Heart Of The Sun'] that it got into Pseud's Corner in *Private Eye* on the strength of it! I wrote a whole bunch of stuff about dying galaxies, which I think I'd actually stolen from a science-fiction book I'd read. But it was really like that, it was just a marvellous performance, and they'd taped it and given me a copy. I used to listen to it every day. Then it was nicked by a discerning burglar some ten years later. It was one of those nights when you were just glad to have been there.'

Top Gear simply went from strength to strength in 1968 – its rise in the ratings seemed unstoppable, with an audience of more than a million listening to music that many felt was far from chart-friendly and very uncommercial. Not bad for its host, who had initially been given only a six-month contract by his new employers.

Peel aimed to have his finger on the pulse of what was happening in the music world, unlike the majority of the other presenters employed by the station, towards whom Peel was often open in his disdain. For many years, Tony Blackburn was a regular target of Peel's stinging criticism. A fellow ex-pirate, Blackburn's was the show that opened Radio One with its first ever record, the Move's 'Flowers In The Rain' (Peel also disliked the Move). The toothsome 'Tone' was a personality-led DJ, a great favourite with housewives, who told bad jokes and stuck rigorously to the station playlist. To cap it all, the former singer even had the temerity to release a series of horrendously commercial records in the late 1960s. To John Peel, he was unworthy of airtime, while his formulaic show, by no means untypical of Radio One's daytime programming, was of little interest to the average Peel follower. Nevertheless his path and John's would regularly cross – even as late as 2002, when Blackburn's success on reality TV show *I'm A Celebrity, Get Me Out Of Here!* led to a brief resumption of 'hostilities' between the two.

For people who listened regularly to *Top Gear*, it was like entering the music academy of their dreams. However, they didn't tune in just for casual enjoyment – they could learn something new. It was a test for his discerning listeners. The range of stuff Peel played was breathtaking. In one three-hour stint, he might broadcast the pop sounds of Birmingham's Idle Race, whose leader Jeff Lynne later led the Electric Light Orchestra, and whose music could take you into a parallel universe reminiscent of the Rupert Bear books. This was presented side-by-side with groups such as the Nice – featuring keyboardist Keith Emerson and, at the time, one of the most exciting live acts around – who, in the space of a year, went from playing psychedelic rock, jazz and folk to full-blown classical interpretations. Their tour de force was a rambunctious version of Leonard Bernstein's 'America', during which Emerson stuck knives into his Hammond organ while the rest of the group burned the American flag. The next moment, Peel would entertain his listeners with the laid-back white blues of Chicken Shack and Fleetwood Mac, both of whom delivered their music with a welcome tongue-in-cheek humour.

The self-styled minor princeling among the hippies was not just content with the role of broadcaster, but he also wrote for a number of publications. He penned a regular column for *International Times* under the *Perfumed Garden* banner and also wrote a monthly contribution to *Disc & Music Echo*, in which he covered acts that included his American favourites the Misunderstood – still going despite all the setbacks. He was also in demand as a writer of sleevenotes and helped out many diverse acts, ranging from Mick Farren and the Social Deviants to folk-rockers Forest.

Eventually, even TV beckoned. Indeed, in 1968, as one of the regular pundits on the alternative arts show *How It Is,*

Peel met his second wife, Sheila Gilhooly, who was a member of the studio audience. The musical content was restricted to just one act per show, though these live slots were far from forgettable, with Led Zeppelin making their UK TV debut with a storming 'Communication Breakdown' and Fairport Convention with Sandy Denny delivering a delightful, anthemic 'Meet On The Ledge'.

The shows covered topics as diverse as the Aquarian-Age musical *Hair*, 1960s supermodel Twiggy and the Beatles' animated feature-length movie *Yellow Submarine*. Angela Huth was the presenter, while figures such as *Oz* editor Richard Neville and women's liberation spokeswoman Germaine Greer appeared regularly. It should be mentioned in passing that Peel, then between marriages, enjoyed a single night of passion with Greer that remained their secret for some two decades . . . and then resulted in accusation and counter-accusation via the press.

It might have surprised the corporate bosses at Brain-washing House (as the Bonzo Dog Doo-Dah Band leader Viv Stanshall later jocularly termed Broadcasting House) when Peel won the first of many awards as Top British DJ and *Top Gear* was voted Best Radio Programme in the annual *Melody Maker* Readers' Poll in September 1968, but for those in the know his shows were an oasis in the desert of pop (or was it pap?) that Radio One broadcast most of the time. And by then he had the added momentum of a second show – one that was far more esoteric, experimental and even more breathtakingly eclectic than *Top Gear*.

In January 1968, John Muir of the Recorded Programmes Department at the Beeb told controller Robin Scott that he wanted to launch something more akin to Peel's original *Perfumed Garden* format to fill the regular *Night Ride* slot between midnight and 1 a.m. on Wednesdays. The first broadcast went out on 6 March, Peel announcing it as 'The first of a new series of programmes on which you may hear just about anything.' Compared to his regular Sunday afternoon show, this was indeed left-field stuff and caused more than a little confusion with fans of more conservative bands such as Deep Purple, Free, Taste and Family, all of whom were *Top Gear* regulars. The main thrust of the new show was to combine folk and poetry with what would now be termed world-music recordings – Peel soon got into the swing of this, digging out gems from the BBC Sound Archive so that, on any given Wednesday, you might hear a session from one of the Liverpool poets such as Adrian Mitchell, songs by a singer-guitarist like Jackson C. Frank or Michael Chapman, and the sound of an African jew's harp made from the body of a live beetle! Into an already eclectic mix, Peel threw in a seasoning of political commentary and discussion on the issues of the day.

The show ran from March 1968 through to September 1969, its time slot moving at one point to the earlier time of 8.15–9.15 p.m., but *Night Ride* is now forgotten by all but Peel's staunchest fans. A shame, for it was a veritable treasure trove of delights – seminal folk acts such as Shirley and Dolly Collins and John Martyn made their debuts on it – while regulars included the Liverpool Scene, Fairport Convention and Roy Harper (again!). There has never been anything like it on the Beeb since: where else could you hear Son House's 'Death Letter' or the avant-garde rantings of Ron Geesin, the first of many sessions by Scottish poet Ivor Cutler (another perennial Peel favourite) or the warm, husky warblings of singer Bridget St John, who would record for Peel's Dandelion label? And it was over successive editions of *Night Ride* that the British public first heard the wonders of what has since been recognized as one of rock's greatest masterpieces, Captain Beefheart and his Magic Band's *Trout Mask Replica*.

Night Ride was regarded as controversial at the time, its contributors including satirical cartoonist Ralph Steadman and *Private Eye*'s John Wells. It was the latter who set the cat among the pigeons when he commented about the then Prime Minister Harold Wilson having no interest in the war in Nigeria as it was a potential vote-loser. There was outrage at 10 Downing Street, and pressure was brought for an apology – Peel was exonerated, the transcript having revealed no more than a series of 'ums' and 'errs' – but Big Brother was now clearly keeping a close eye on the show.

The clergy were the next group to take offence: after John Lennon and Yoko Ono came in and played a cassette of their unborn baby's heartbeat over the air (sadly Ono was later to miscarry), the Reverend John McNicol complained that the broadcast was a 'stunt' in bad taste. Another edition of the programme, which touched on the dangers of sexually transmitted disease, further enraged the establishment, especially when Peel announced that he had once caught VD and that there should be more public awareness about it.

Despite some incredible later sessions by luminaries such as the Floyd (their last studio outing for the BBC, in fact), the show inevitably came to an end. The final *Night Ride* went out on Wednesday 24 September 1969. Its death knell was sounded by Bob Dylan whose vitriolic epic 'Desolation Row' from the *Highway 61 Revisited* LP closed proceedings on a dramatic, defiant and bitter note. Back then it was a radical and very brave step for a public body such as the BBC to back such a programme. Nowadays the establishment would be unlikely to commission something like it in the first place.

Despite this setback, late 1968 and all of 1969 would further consolidate John's position as a major arbiter of public taste and promoter of great music: on Sunday afternoons he previewed tracks from the Pretty Things' magnificent rock opera *SF Sorrow* (inspiration for the Who's *Tommy*), the Beatles' *White Album* and the Rolling Stones' latest LP, *Beggars Banquet*. The early part of 1969 saw debuts by such underground heavyweights as Colosseum, Caravan and Led Zeppelin, plus the first of several sets from politically motivated heavy rockers the Edgar Broughton Band.

In February the show pulled off something of a coup by getting a session with San Francisco legends Moby Grape, who were touring Europe but who sadly broke up soon after. Peel was a huge fan of Bay Area bands – he had been the first DJ in England to play material by Quicksilver Messenger Service and was a huge champion of the Grateful Dead. Listeners were regularly treated to tracks from albums such as the Dead's *Anthem Of The Sun* and *Aoxomoxoa*, while the DJ would have the privilege of introducing the group at the Hollywood Pop Festival near Stoke-on-Trent in May 1970, which marked their British debut. (Compèring festivals would become a regular activity for Peel over the years, most notably and regularly at Reading and Glastonbury.)

In 1969, the BBC would honour their new protégé by releasing not one but two albums bearing Peel's name. One was his selection of tracks from the BBC Sound Archive, which had gone down a storm with *Night Ride* aficionados, the second a *Top Gear* LP – though anybody expecting the hard-rock bands regularly aired on the latter programme would be in for a shock. The nearest they got to conventional rock was a band from Manchester called Sweet Marriage, the rest of the album featuring some beautiful tracks from Bridget St John (including a stunning version of Joni Mitchell's 'Night In The City'), as well as more radical contributions from the Welfare State and Ron Geesin. One of the highlights was hearing Peel's voice electronically treated by Delia Derbyshire of the BBC Radiophonic Workshop. All in all, though, it was more *Night Ride* than *Top Gear*.

Changes were very definitely afoot at the time. On a global scale, the highs of Woodstock in the summer of 1969 were quickly followed by a murder at the Altamont Pop Festival in California, which indicated the demise of the hippie ideal. Closer to home, Peel favourites Fairport Convention suffered a van crash in which their drummer Martin Lamble and guitarist Richard Thompson's girlfriend Jeannie Franklin were both killed. Peel was reportedly seen wearing a black armband in mourning at the Roundhouse the next day. He'd later help out at various benefit gigs for the band and gave them their finest-ever testimonial in his *Disc* column that June, reviewing their newest album, *Unhalfbricking* in the most glowing of terms, and proclaiming 'Fairport Convention we love you!'

Peel once described himself as a catalyst, and he was certainly somebody who made things happen. That summer saw him set up his own independent label, Dandelion, in partnership with ex-Elektra Records (UK) boss Clive Selwood, the man who had been involved with putting on the 1960 Eddie Cochran and Gene Vincent tour that so influenced Peel at the time. But the most important event of 1969 in John Peel's professional life came in April when his close and rewarding relationship with Bernie Andrews was suddenly brought to an end. If anybody had encouraged John to be himself, it was Bernie. And in retrospect it seems something of an injustice that Andrews's contribution to John's career has received far less acclaim than the DJ's work with John Walters, the man who would become his next producer.

The Beeb decided that Andrews should not concentrate solely on one programme but, like his peers, also take on general duties. He was assigned Radio Two's *Music While You Work*, something he saw as too much of a clash of interest and which also increased his workload. Inevitably, he was forced to quit *Top Gear* – though not before getting the Nice to produce an updated version of the show's theme tune, originally recorded by Sounds Incorporated. This heavily echoed reworking by organist Keith Emerson was to become Peel's theme until October 1975, when he replaced it with Southern boogie band Grinderswitch's simple 'Pickin' The Blues'.

John Walters's arrival as producer was initially, and understandably, greeted by a degree of resentment and suspicion on Peel's part. Born and bred in Derbyshire, Walters had settled in the north-east during his university days, and it was while living in Newcastle – lecturing in jazz studies and writing a jazz column for a local paper – that he met Alan Price, former keyboard player with the Animals. He joined the Alan Price Set in 1965 and played trumpet for the band for three years before deciding that working for the BBC might be an easier option. As he later reminisced in *ZigZag*: 'From what I'd seen of the BBC studios, they seemed full of people doing nothing at all, and it looked like money for old rope. Having been involved with the pop business for some time, I thought I must have some knowledge of it and wrote to them.'

Walters had to wait a while after his job interview before getting a foot in the door when 'wonderful' Radio One was launched in September 1967. Initially attached to the weekly magazine-style show *Scene and Heard*, Walters got his break working with one of the station's most popular figures, Jimmy Savile. The cigar-smoking, exotically dressed personality had decided he wanted to do a show in which he went round Britain talking to people. Walters was assigned as producer and immediately came up with its snappy title, *Savile's Travels*.

Of course, the quietly spoken Peel was the complete antithesis of Jimmy and, as Walters recalled, this added to his antipathy. 'Peelie disliked me intensely because, to him, I represented a form of cynicism and commercialism from the Savile era. When Peelie and I got together, we were both, for different reasons, aghast. I'd seen the more superficial side of the underground thing and thought it was all that "running through the cornfields of my mind" sort of piss because there was so much of that "margarine policeman" stuff after *Sgt Pepper*. Naturally I reacted strongly against this, whereas Peelie was a bit more committed. He hoped it would develop into a more mature side.

'While I took the piss out of it, he encouraged it in the hope that something would happen, so we were at different ends,' Walters reflected. 'But eventually we broke it down, had a couple of lunches together and found that we had more in common than we thought because we tend to laugh at the same things. I think the turning point came when I noticed that there was a W. C. Fields festival on at somewhere like the Baker Street Times cinema and he wasn't keen to go until I told him what was on; he'd been an admirer of W. C. Fields for years, and so we went. We went back to his flat for coffee, and suddenly realized that we were both concerned in some ways about the quality of the rock scene.'

While Peel had believed in much of the underground ideology, he could increasingly see the downside of it. He once remarked, 'The only time I took acid voluntarily was at UFO. It was jolly nice. I've always rather flippantly said since that it was rather like going to Stratford-upon-Avon: once you've done it I didn't see the need to do it again.'

Though it switched to a Saturday-afternoon slot in autumn 1969, *Top Gear*, with Walters at the desk, changed very little to begin with. For example, one show in September 1969 featured a quite brilliant session from the revitalized Fairport Convention. They were just entering their most creative period, pioneering a type of folk-rock that equalled anything by their US counterparts the Band or the Byrds, and the session saw them play traditional numbers like 'Matty Groves' and 'Reynardine' that would feature later on their classic *Liege And Lief* LP. Meanwhile, the awards kept on coming both for Peel and the programme, not only from readers of *Melody Maker* but also *Disc & Music Echo*.

Slowly but surely, however, *Top Gear* began to change. There were definitely two sides to Peel. His sensitive side saw him eloquently hold forth on a topic such as the small furry denizens of London Zoo's Moonlight World, discuss the state of being lonely or espouse the qualities of healthy eating – he was an avowed vegetarian. Yet there was always a bit of a laddish aspect to him, years before the term was popularized. While he had initially believed without question in the hippie vision, he'd later admit: 'It was terrible vanity but I thought that we would be responsible for the moral advance that would match the technological advance of the previous hundred years. Quite clearly, it came to bugger all.'

The rot that set into his relationship with the alternative society seemed to accelerate at the launch of Dandelion: 'It was all very idealistic,' he told writer Jonathan Green. 'The chap who started it and myself were taking no money out of it. We had a vegetarian reception for the music business, without any alcohol at all; all these case-hardened old drunks turned up and were absolutely speechless with fury. We had a special presentation box with about four singles in it, a paper dandelion and a few other bits and pieces – so I rushed round to *International Times* and *Oz* and [hippie record shop] Gandalf's Garden and so on – but none of them would review the records because there was no advertising in this. I was very downcast, and that was when the process of disillusionment in the hippie thing began for me.'

As well as the music, he was always eager to talk about the beautiful game and his beloved Liverpool FC. While many of his hippie peers frowned on taking alcohol, John liked the occasional tipple – over the coming years Walters would help bring out this side of his character. Moreover, over time the humour would become more scathing – it's no surprise that the first time many people heard about *Monty Python's Flying Circus* was through *Top Gear*. A tougher, less tolerant Peel was about to emerge. Whether through disillusionment with the counter-culture, or simply a decision to be true to himself, John was ready for the new decade.

5

Sounds of the Seventies

THE TRANSITION from sunshine 1960s to grey, workaday 1970s was a difficult one for music to make – something that was mirrored both in the fortunes of Radio One and those who played the music it broadcast. John Peel was to become one of the few people working in the arena of popular music who made a smooth transition between the two decades.

Few new bands were breaking through – or at least, few totally new bands. The Faces, for instance, had evolved from the Small Faces after lead singer Steve Marriott had quit to form supergroup Humble Pie with Peter Frampton. Former gravedigger Rod Stewart, who'd achieved a degree of fame as vocalist with the Jeff Beck Group in the 1960s, was the man selected as Marriott's replacement. In truth he was lucky to be there at all. He had only accompanied fellow ex-Beck man Ronnie Wood to rehearsals at the Rolling Stones' Bermondsey complex 'on spec', but after he arrived he had been asked to sing a few numbers with ex-Small Faces

Ronnie Lane (bass), Ian McLagan (organ) and Kenney Jones (drums). 'We were quite pathetic at singing,' admitted McLagan, 'so it was a case of having to get a singer. But we didn't want to get into the situation where he'd be the front man and we'd just end up playing behind him.'

That, of course, would turn out to be the case a few years along the line, but the group's 'all-lads-together' ethos was appealing to Peel, and the Faces were to loom large in his life for a number of years. They vigorously espoused the bachelor lifestyle – Rod Stewart would make a career of it, even when married – and their preference of booze to dope as a stimulant of choice mirrored Peel's own recreational leanings. 'Come an' have a drink, you old fart' was their invitation, and he was happy to oblige. Eventually. 'I was a very serious hippie when I met the Faces backstage at one of their concerts,' John later recalled. 'I felt absolutely shocked, sober and precious when they stumbled out of their dressing room, loud, vulgar and very Cockney . . . When they stormed down the hall and disappeared I realized they were having a lot more fun than I was. Next time they invited me [for a drink], I went along.' The Faces were also the only band to make John Peel dance . . . 'and I'm a person who *never* dances. Never, never, never.' Indeed, the Faces performed at what Peel, fully three decades later, was still calling his 'best-ever gig' – at the Sunderland Locarno in early April 1973, the night the local football team beat mighty Arsenal, one division their superior, in the semi-final of the FA Cup before going on to win the competition.

Lindisfarne, from nearby Newcastle, were one band that took advantage of the dearth of exciting new names around, and even topped the album chart almost by default in March 1972 with their album *Fog On The Tyne*. (They fended off all comers for a month before Deep Purple's *Fireball* restored some semblance of order.) The group owed their popularity not only to Peel's patronage but also their participation in the Six Bob Tour (the brainchild of Charisma label boss and impresario Tony Stratton-Smith), which coupled three 'next-big-thing' bands – Van Der Graaf Generator and some outfit called Genesis – in the fashion of the package tours of the 1960s. Lindisfarne's 'in' with *Top Gear* was the Tyneside origins of John Walters. Drummer Ray Laidlaw told Ken Garner of the 'very enjoyable relationship' they enjoyed with him, and recalled that they were told to 'Whack down any old shit [for the session], it all sounds the same to me anyway'.

Though the era of the American hippie festival – most famously exemplified by Monterey and Woodstock in 1967 and 1969 respectively – was long gone, the atmosphere soured irrevocably by the violence wrought by the Hell's Angels at Altamont, Britain began belatedly to catch on. The Isle of Wight festivals of 1969 and 1970 that had attracted such names as Hendrix, Dylan and Joni Mitchell, gave way to rather less exotic events, and certainly when John headed for the Glastonbury Fayre of 1971 it was unlikely that either he or farmer Michael Eavis, on whose land it was staged, could have anticipated what it was the start of. Glastonbury's first pyramid stage was constructed from scaffolding and expanded metal covered with plastic sheeting, and built on a site above the Glastonbury–Stonehenge ley line. A crowd estimated at 12,000 enjoyed music from the likes of Hawkwind, Traffic, Melanie, David Bowie, Joan Baez and Fairport Convention – and admission was free!

Back at the Beeb, Peel didn't really get behind the wave of heavy metal led by bands like Black Sabbath, although he had given that group their first and only Radio One session in November 1969. 'Behind The Wall Of Sleep', 'NIB', 'Black Sabbath' and 'Devil's Island' were consigned to tape at that session, though the last track was eventually to be broadcast in March 1970. The 'leg-up' did get Peel a heartfelt tribute from Ozzy Osbourne in 2004, though: 'He was a pioneer in his own right. If it wasn't for John Peel, Black Sabbath would never have been played on the radio. He was a good guy.'

In the main, though, Peel was very much against the superstar lifestyle lived and expounded on by the likes of Sabbath, Deep Purple, Emerson Lake and Palmer, and Ten Years After. 'They're basically going through a routine,' he moaned to *Melody Maker* in early 1971. 'They've lost the spark somewhere down the line . . . we're going though a very sterile period.' He also hated the term 'progressive rock', which was used by some of the less obviously metallic outfits of the time, claiming that it was a contradiction in terms, 'because if it does [progress] then people don't want to know'.

Peel and Walters decided a more fruitful avenue of musical exploration lay in jazz-rock, with groups such as Ian Carr's Nucleus and Chris McGregor's Brotherhood of Breath featuring in session. Carr told author Ken Garner of his delight that they had 'more artistic freedom on these non-jazz programmes. Nobody seemed to worry about how long each piece was or whether it was the "right sort" of piece for the programme.'

Soft Machine were also operating in this area and had considerably more crossover potential to a rock audience. So into the *Top Gear* concept were they that singer/drummer Robert Wyatt even ad-libbed new lyrics to their song 'Moon In June', which made reference to the programme, recommending it 'despite its extraordinary name' and name-checking 'mates like Kevin [Ayers], Caravan and the old Pink Floyd'. Wyatt later explained that the original lyrics had been written as a joke that had worn thin by the time they arrived at Maida Vale, so he simply wrote new ones on the spot.

That was in 1969. Four years later, Wyatt was to suffer a fall from a fourth-floor window that would leave him wheelchair-bound and unable to drum or tour. The Peel sessions he recorded while attempting, successfully, to launch a solo career were, he'd later admit, truly cathartic experiences. September 1974, for instance, had seen him come in on his own to assay versions of songs, including the hit Monkees' cover 'I'm A Believer', with minimal instrumentation. He knew he didn't have to worry: artistic freedom was a given, with Peel never someone to insist that the session should bear any relation to the original recording.

The summer of 1971 had seen Wyatt and bandmate of the time, Mike Ratledge, roped in as part of a John Walters experimental 'free improvisation' session. The idea was to utilize the 'talents' of two performing chimpanzees playing the piano, much as mathematician Emile Borel had put monkeys at typewriters in the hope of eventually producing literature. Unlikely as it may seem, John Lennon and Yoko Ono offered their services alongside the jew's harp of Peel and then-girlfriend Sheila. Unfortunately, Lennon's decision to remain in the States scuppered the session, though a New York picture postcard from him that read 'Hold on to the chimps' arrived *chez* Walters some weeks later.

In an unrelated development, Peel and Walters organized a kind of prehistoric *Pop Idol* competition in which the best two demo tapes won a Peel session. Henry Cow, an avant-garde outfit of Cambridge University students (sample song title: 'Poglith Drives A Vauxhall Viva'), won in the group category and went on to enjoy a low-key career on Virgin Records. The winners of the duo category were not Bugsy and Rosie the performing chimps, but guitarists and vocalists Paul Savage and John Hewitt – of whom nothing was ever heard again.

At the time, much was heard on Radio One of Peel

protégé Bob Harris, a softly spoken policeman's son who had co-founded the London listings magazine *Time Out* before opting for a career in broadcasting. He'd first met John when a student journalist, and had hit it off so well that regularly thereafter he sought out his mentor for advice. Flattered, Peel featured him in his column in the *Disc & Music Echo*, one of the leading music weeklies – or 'inkies', as the tabloid-format papers were known. One described a visit from Bob and first wife Sue in the early 1970s at which, after a 'complex football/tennis game Bob and I played 'til we could hardly stand', the DJs consumed a repast fashioned by their 'old ladies'. They then headed out to scour junk shops in Ipswich for obscure 45s, their partners still presumably in tow.

Interestingly, by 1972 Harris was being described in *Melody Maker* as 'John Peel's natural successor, in that he has cemented a firm relationship between himself and his audience with music as his primary justification. Of how many Radio One DJs could you say that?' Yet while this compliment was well deserved, Harris's musical tastes would remain remarkably constant over the years, whereas Peel was always striving to be contemporary even if it meant alienating a section of his listening public – as would become very apparent in a few short years.

Peel's performing causes célèbres of the early 1970s included two particularly offbeat characters in the form of Ivor Cutler and Lol Coxhill. Cutler, who was to record eighteen sessions for Peel between 1969 and 1991, was a wizened Scots poet apt to noodle away on the harmonium, while Coxhill was a former busker who had played in Kevin Ayers's Whole World and specialized in atonal saxophone playing that, in this writer's humble opinion, could strip paint from walls. Not that one would have said as much to the face of such a burly, shaven-headed individual . . .

Another unusual performer who would have been unlikely to find the audience he did without Peel's patronage (and was still saying so from the stage recently) was American singer and raconteur Loudon Wainwright III. He even made his home in London in the early 1970s, and was rewarded with the bulk of his ten Peel sessions. Again, the DJ stayed loyal to the performer, recording him until 1989.

Though Peel would host *Top of the Pops* many times in the 1980s, he owed his most famous appearance on the programme to the Faces. His reward for championing their music was to sit on a chair with a mandolin and self-consciously strum along to the chart-topping single 'Maggie May', which began a five-week stretch at number one on 9 October 1971. The clip, replayed countless times since, saw Stewart and his band turn to Peel as he mimed the closing mandolin solo (played on the record by Ray 'Jacka' Jackson from *Top Gear* regulars Lindisfarne). They then royally sent up the whole process by abandoning the charade to conduct a football game between themselves; Peel and drummer Kenney Jones the only men to remain at their posts.

The problem for the Faces was that 'Maggie May' and its parent album *Every Picture Tells A Story*, which made history by topping the UK and US listings, were in fact Rod Stewart solo recordings, even if the Faces played greater or lesser roles as sidemen on them. And this would prove the beginning of a process of disintegration that saw Ronnie Wood exit to join the Rolling Stones, initially on loan, and Stewart abandon Britain and his old friends (including Peel) for a playboy life in the States: the title of his 1975 album *Atlantic Crossing* was as accurate as it was symbolic. Thus the heyday of Rod and John's friendship was destined to last for only a few years, though at least his association with the Faces helped Peel to assuage some of the boredom the early 1970s music scene seemed to radiate. Glam rock, to which Peel protégé Marc Bolan had gravitated, held no allure for a man well on his way into his fourth decade and now sporting a full-time beard rather than mutton-chop whiskers.

Peel was very excited by one band of mascara-wearers, though: Roxy Music, who burst on to the scene in 1971, thanks to positive press coverage from *Melody Maker*'s Richard Williams (also the first presenter of the *Old Grey Whistle Test*, before Bob Harris). Impressed not by their image but, rather, the Velvet Underground-influenced demo tape they'd submitted, Peel made them his first session of 1972. The recording featured ex-Nice guitarist David O'List who would, a month later, be replaced by Phil Manzanera. The group had yet to lay down the tracks for their ground-breaking eponymous debut album.

Changes at Radio One in October 1971 moved the *Sounds of the Seventies* programmes (of which *Top Gear* was one) to a 10 p.m.-to-midnight slot. Peel began with a Wednesday night show and, early in the new year, acquired Friday nights, his midweek programme briefly moving to Tuesday. Each show was to feature two artists or bands in session, which led to considerable employment opportunities for engineers and producers. John Walters bowed out of session production around this time, leaving the lion's share to one Tony Wilson (no relation to the Manchester mogul behind Factory Records and the Haçienda).

October 1972 was a landmark in Radio One history: the station became a self-contained twenty-four-hours-a-day channel (previously, certain hours of the night had been shared with Radio Two). Peel's show was shifted to Thursday nights, and his partnership with Bernie Andrews briefly reinstated. Again, though, little new talent was showing itself, and Andrews's fourteen months as producer would see only a dozen new bands make their radio debuts. Prominent among these were Richard and Linda Thompson (the former a veteran of many a Fairport Convention session), Camel and Queen.

Interestingly, Queen's first two sessions were aired on the Thursday night shows in 1973, but as the group soared up the career ladder the next three were recorded for Bob Harris. Yet in a move that must have made Peel chuckle with pleasure, they would express their gratitude for the early 'leg-up' by coming back to record a Peel session in October 1977, at the peak of the punk era.

Early 1973 had seen John Peel and the Faces back out on the razzle to celebrate the conclusion of the group's fourth album, *Ooh-La-La*. It wasn't a record Rod Stewart, in particular, with one eye on his solo career, would claim much affection for, though the title track, penned by Ronnie Wood and the criminally underrated Ronnie 'Plonk' Lane, has since become something of an old rocker's anthem, with its distinctive, lyrical quality of sadness and nostalgia.

The band returned to London to play a promotional show at the Paris Theatre in Lower Regent Street to be broadcast by Radio One and compèred, naturally, by Peel. Over to Ronnie Wood: 'We used to have the greatest time with that Liverpool supporter, John Peel,' he slurred. 'He was great to go round the pub with and get totally pissed, then back to the BBC studios and go out live on air. Never having any idea about the set list or who was doing what, giving each other piggy-back rides to the stage, with Ronnie Lane always on my or Rod's back.' The BBC wasn't quite as foolish as it seemed, in fact, and broadcast the concert a couple of weeks later rather than risk the Faces blotting their copybook on live national radio. In truth, it's doubtful any of them knew or cared.

In complete contrast to the Faces' boozy rock, electronic-based (and often melody-free) 'Krautrock' music from Germany enjoyed something of a heyday at this time thanks to our man. Peel championed multi-instrumental duo Neu! to the delight of a young listener called Julian Cope, who confessed that his 'attitude to all music changed' as a result, while Can were also regulars on the show, along with fellow countrymen Faust and Tangerine Dream. The latter, piloted then as now by perfectionist Edgar Froese, preferred to send in their own tapes for broadcast rather than subject themselves to the BBC's stick-and-string studios.

Robert Fripp and Brian Eno, cutting themselves adrift from King Crimson and Roxy Music respectively, took the Krautrock route for their collaborations, and Peel (who'd ditched Crimson after two 1969 sessions as they became too progressive 'with a capital P') was happy to broadcast the results. Unfortunately, a December 1973 broadcast brought disaster after Fripp and Eno also elected to supply a tape of their own. The BBC had the custom of storing tapes 'front out' rather than 'tail out', the industry standard, with the result that the album *No Pussyfooting* was broadcast backwards. John Walters recalls that Eno was the only listener who noticed, although the BBC switchboard refused to put him through to the studio when he pulled into a motorway services and called in to rectify the situation. In Peel and Walters's defence, the two extended tracks that comprised the album were highly experimental even when played the correct way!

John could also take partial credit for rescuing the then fledgling Virgin Records. Peel played the obscure Mike Oldfield's *Tubular Bells* in its entirety on his programme, giving the record, Virgin's first release, the boost it needed to eventually propel it to the number-one spot on the British charts. 'The finest record I've heard in many years' was the man's considered verdict. (Ironically, when it came time for the reclusive Oldfield to premiere the work live, he chose as his backing group 1971 Peel 'talent-contest' winners Henry Cow.) Richard Branson and Peel were never, however, the greatest of buddies.

A seasonal flavour had been a traditional part of Peel's festive programming since a choir had been convened in 1970 to sing carols for the Boxing Day edition of *Top Gear*. The assembled multitude on that occasion had included Marc Bolan, the Faces, Sonja Kristina of Curved Air, Mike Ratledge from Soft Machine, and Ivor Cutler. In 1973 it was Elton John's turn to transform the studio into a 'local' and reprise the period of his life when he'd played Jim Reeves and Ray Charles ballads at Pinner's Northwood Hills Hotel on weekends for pocket money.

There was an intentional humour to the whole event: the year had seen Elton finally break through to multi-platinum status with the album *Goodbye Yellow Brick Road* after four years as a recording artist – and many years of struggle before that. Interestingly, he'd never done a studio session with Peel, though the latter had presented a 1970 *Elton John In Concert* show.

Like Peel, Elton had a passion for football – in his case, Watford FC – and a terraces atmosphere was encouraged by the importation of crates of beer to the tiny studio in Egton House. Peel, Walters and sundry Radio One production personnel gathered around the upright piano and lent their voices lustily to the finale, a version of Elton's hit 'Your Song'. As well as a medley of seasonal favourites including 'Rudolf The Red Nosed Reindeer', 'White Christmas' and 'Jingle Bells', Elton took on Dylan's 'Mr Tambourine Man', 'Blowin' In the Wind' and 'She Belongs To Me' (in another medley) as well as his own 'Daniel'. All this was broadcast on Christmas Day to the background of clinking bottles and Walters acting the pub landlord with the appropriate calls of 'Last orders!' and 'Time, gentlemen, please!'

Joan Armatrading adopted a very similar singer-songwriter style to Elton – indeed, the two of them shared the same producer in Gus Dudgeon. Peel had actually attended her first session in 1972, and had been so impressed that he would commission seven more from her in the next four years. During this time she would blossom from a shy girl who barely spoke into an international star, though his approval would remain important to her. Indeed, she told *In Session Tonight* author Ken Garner of her joy on seeing a positive review by him of her appearance at Amnesty International's fundraiser *The Secret Policeman's Third Ball* in 1987: 'Peel gave me a great review and that pleased me immensely because sometimes if he likes you, then you have success and stop doing the show, you think he doesn't like you anymore . . . I've always considered him a big part of my career; I know some people wouldn't think so, but I do.'

Peel had a penchant for folky singer-songwriters and had a set of favourites he'd regularly call in for sessions. One was Scotsman Robert 'Rab' Noakes, who'd coincidentally penned a number of tunes for Lindisfarne in their early days. Another was Martin Carthy. Noakes later became a radio producer himself, so perhaps he picked up a few hints from the master. Folk groups as diverse as the High Level Ranters and Albion Country Band were also given a welcome opportunity to escape their specialist niches.

And that wasn't the only niche music John Peel was exploring in the early 1970s. To the British, reggae was a genre of music synonymous with novelty records such as Desmond Dekker's 'Israelites', and was often dismissed as 'skinhead music'. Peel had no such qualms – and proved it by giving Bob Marley his first major UK radio exposure. The Wailers still numbered future solo stars Bunny Livingston and Peter Tosh in their ranks when they and their marijuana cigarettes first permeated the BBC's rarefied atmosphere in May 1973. John Walters reflected that his Corporation training suggested he called the police when he caught them 'spliffing up'. But what stuck in his memory more than the sweet smell of excess was Marley's quiet dignity: 'You realized he was a star.' There would be a second session later in the year, by which time Bunny Livingston had quit en route to solo success as Bunny Wailer. Tosh would soon follow, leaving Marley the undisputed figurehead and embodiment of reggae to millions of people worldwide.

Marley was on his way onwards and upwards, away from the world of the Peel session, but John found many a band to take his place. Future chart-toppers Aswad were particular favourites in their early, rawer incarnation, but his biggest passion was reserved for Misty In Roots. The West London-based collective who released tracks on their own People Unite label made no fewer than eight Peel session appearances between 1979 and 1986, while another session was recorded for Peel's 'rhythm pal' David Jensen, on whom John's taste had clearly rubbed off.

Peel remained resolutely at odds with the 'Smashie and Nicey' stereotype of Radio One DJs, and more or less declined to fraternize with them. 'It's just not my sort of thing,' he'd later confess with pride, before telling a story against himself. 'I remember Mike Read once taking me to some terrifically trendy club off Bond Street, and he was immediately surrounded by all sorts of glamorous women. It was one of those places where they have an area where only top celebs can go, and Bryan Ferry came down and was doing a walkabout, as if he were talking to schoolchildren clutching flags. I could see him looking across this glamorous crowd at me, with me looking like the man who'd come to collect the empties.'

On an earlier occasion he somehow found himself at fellow DJ Dave Lee Travis's house and, as any self-respecting music-lover would, made a beeline towards his record collection. Or rather he attempted to, for there appeared to be a complete absence of vinyl in the Travis household. On interrogating the self-styled 'Hairy Cornflake', Peel was told, 'Anything I really like I've copied on tape and play in the car . . .' For a man who built an extension to his house to accommodate his LP collection, this must have been hard to understand. (As one might expect, Peel would later be scathing about the CD format.)

In the early 1970s, Peel was critical of the output of his channel, and it's inconceivable any other DJ could have broken ranks in such a way without being summarily dismissed. 'You can listen to Radio One for an entire week – a year even,' he once complained, 'and you won't hear anything at all that relates to anything that's going on . . . it's just all incredibly predictable, sort of porridge, really . . . just meaningless.'

Yet his status as a mainstay of 'wonderful Radio One', as the jingles had it, did have the occasional worthwhile spin-off. The *John Peel Roadshow* was a very important part of his life in the 1970s – not least because it augmented his BBC income which, for the amount of work he put in, was definitely at civil-servant levels. In an attempt to add a little glamour to his shows on the road he even employed a pair of go-go girls for a while, whom he described as, 'A couple of young women from Luton who thought it was going to be real showbiz and they'd get to meet Noel Edmonds and stuff.' The arrangement would turn out to be a temporary measure, as Peel remarked, 'They were sorely disappointed'; perhaps the experience was not quite what the girls had been expecting,

Thus it was that Peel, the self-styled 'King of the Polytechnics', spent much of his time in a Land Rover-based camper van cruising the highways and byways. But the roadshow days would draw to a close once the Ravenscroft brood started appearing later in the decade: 'I thought I'd be more use to them here than sleeping in a lay-by somewhere on the A1.' (He'd later suggest that this lifestyle and the diet that accompanied it might have caused the diabetes he suffered from in later life.)

Family life was clearly something that rated high in Peel's list of values. And it was pal Bob Harris's apparent disregard for the needs of his own wife, Sue, and their daughters Mirelle and Emily that led to a major rift between the once mutually supportive pair. Indeed, Harris revealed in his biography *The Whispering Years*, published in 2001, that he and Peel did not exchange a word for almost twenty years after their dramatic falling out. 'I was a married man living a single man's life,' Harris confessed. 'It was beginning to mix badly with commitments at home, and I was rolling in too late too many nights.' Peel, who was very fond of Sue 'began to express his disapproval', and soon after Harris started the *Old Grey Whistle Test*, the TV music programme with which he was to become synonymous, the pair stopped talking altogether. The crunch came when Bob was 'blanked' in the corridor at Egton House. He ran back to accost his former friend and pulled him into an empty office, but Peel 'wouldn't look at me' and 'stared at the floor, impassive . . . eventually I just had to let him walk out of there, our friendship in ruins.'

The mid-1970s was a very uncomfortable period to be a BBC employee at Radio One. The balance sheet for the corporation, funded then as now by the BBC's licence fee, was some £20 million out of whack, and there would have to be economies aplenty. The contracts of many of the old guard of DJs would not be renewed when they expired. Thus the likes of Alan Black, Bob Harris and Stuart Henry were released – and as Harris bitterly commented to *Melody Maker*, 'The only real survivor will be *Top Gear*.'

With Radios One and Two once more sharing common programming for economy's sake, Peel found himself in an unusual early-evening slot on Mondays and Thursdays, a strange state of affairs that lasted from February to September 1975; Alan Freeman, Anne Nightingale and Emperor Rosko filled the corresponding Tuesday, Wednesday and Friday positions. But they had no session capability, which meant that opportunities for new or unsigned bands to get airplay were now more limited than ever.

It all changed again at the end of September when the powers that be finally fell in with *Melody Maker*'s assertion that strangling *Sounds of the Seventies* to save less than half a million pounds a year, given the total corporation budget of £140 million, was unreasonable. Peel was the beneficiary, claiming the final hour from 11 p.m. to midnight on each and every weekday. The benefits of this were soon to be felt by listeners of every age and persuasion: whether you'd just come in from the pub, returned from a gig or simply wanted music to fall asleep to, tuning in and turning on to Peel became an institution a nation shared. That said, he was essentially a lone voice in the wilderness – something that gave him a responsibility he was not to treat lightly.

The pub-rock trend had briefly suggested a new musical route out of the early 1970s rut, and Peel gave it airtime in the shape of Ducks Deluxe, Brinsley Schwarz and Ace, the latter featuring future solo star Paul Carrack. Graham Parker and the Rumour, Roogalator and the Count Bishops also cut energetic Peel sessions in early to mid-1976.

In the end, of course, it would prove the forerunner to punk; Peel faves Eddie and the Hot Rods being perhaps the nearest thing to midwives. Interestingly, fellow Southenders Dr Feelgood made two Peel session appearances in 1975 and 1977, either side of their number-one live album *Stupidity*.

Coincidentally, Peel had been publicly espousing a return to the two-and-a half-minute single for some time, arguing that if Jerry Lee Lewis had said all he needed to say in that time then it should be good enough for the rest of the world. A number of bands he'd championed from the beginning, such as Soft Machine's Canterbury compadres Caravan, were themselves realizing they'd run out of steam (though the ever-loyal Peel gave them a session a year from 1974 to 1977, the year they finally suspended operations). 'At the time, the [press] quote was "Your hair's too long, your trousers are too wide, fuck off!" – and that applied to us,' lead vocalist Pye Hastings conceded to this writer in 2000. 'We'd all got bored trying to play faster and faster, more complicated time signatures . . . it wasn't entertaining.' Caravan would resurface two decades later as a 'classic rock' band, at the other end of the musical spectrum from Peel's cutting-edge programming.

Punk would present its own challenges, not least the fact that Peel and Walters saw it as an either/or choice. To embrace the movement totally would be to alienate many, if not all, of the listener base that Peel had spent the best part of a decade building up. Ken Garner got the story of John's 1976 punk epiphany from the man himself for his book *In Session Tonight*, learning that it was his habit to walk to the Virgin record shop at Marble Arch, down the road from

Broadcasting House, and borrow records 'on approval'. 'One week I took out about ten LPs, one of which was the [eponymous] one by the Ramones. I liked the simplicity of the name, an implication of that romantic Spanish-New York thing; and also because it had a monochrome sleeve.'

Peel would have been surprised to note that 'da brudders' selected the name Ramone to replace their respective surnames purely because that great son of Liverpool, Paul McCartney, used Paul Ramon as a *nom de disque* for recording purposes or to check incognito into a hotel.

On placing the plastic on his turntable, Peel confessed himself 'taken aback' by the 'aggression and brevity of the numbers' but sufficiently excited to play it on his show that same night. So it was that a programme that otherwise featured such solidly middle-of-the-road rock talents as Nils Lofgren, Steve Miller and Family spin-off band Streetwalkers ended with 'Judy Is A Punk'.

At a guess, this could have been a Radio One first for the punk genre, and was swiftly added to the following night, when Peel put the stylus down in the middle of side two and played the album's final three tracks one after the other. This was mid-May. The Ramones famously played the Roundhouse at Chalk Farm on Independence Day, 4 July 1976, a gig attended by almost everyone who would be anyone in the forthcoming punk maelstrom that hit the UK. After that experience, 'Blitzkrieg Bop' was a fixture on the Peel playlist and the revolution was on.

6

Selwood, Sheila
and Shankly

THREE RELATIONSHIPS stood as constants in John Peel's adult life. His manager Clive Selwood, his love for Liverpool Football Club – as exemplified by their craggy Scottish manager Bill Shankly – and his second wife Sheila, whom he met in a TV studio and married six years later in 1974. All three were to be the foundation stones of his life.

Born in 1935, four years before Peel, Clive Selwood could be said to have been a jack-of-all-trades when it came to the number and range of jobs he had had in the British music business. Starting life as a would-be performer (he once shared a stage with child star Petula Clark), he moved behind the scenes, working his way up from the status of on-the-road rep and for several heady years at the end of the 1960s was the British face of Elektra Records when that groundbreaking label boasted such luminaries as the Doors, the Incredible String Band, Love and Tim Buckley.

It was in the summer of 1967 – when, as Elektra general manager, he was promoting the Incredibles' *The 5,000 Spirits*

Or The Layers Of The Onion – that Selwood first encountered Peel. The band, a weird and wonderful collection of raggle-taggle hippie folkies, would probably have been a marketing man's nightmare at any other time than the Summer of Love, but a combination of Selwood's efforts and Peel's patronage – as mentioned earlier, he played both sides straight through on his Radio London show – saw the album in question reach number twenty-six in the charts. (Its early 1968 successor, *The Hangman's Beautiful Daughter*, soared to the unlikely heights of number five.)

When the pirates hit the rocks, Selwood's contacts at the BBC helped oil the wheels to help give John a place on the newly assembled Radio One team. Having achieved this not inconsiderable feat, Clive Selwood found himself the DJ's manager – a role that he (and wife Shurley, an ex-dancer also well versed in the showbiz world) fulfilled until Peel's death. Clive also took on the affairs of Peel's Radio One colleague Johnnie Walker, still broadcasting today albeit on Radio Two, and fellow *Top Gear* founder Pete Drummond.

Selwood's self-confessed *métier*, salesmanship, certainly made up for Peel's unabashed non-commercialism, and would yield his client some much-needed extra cash when voiceovers and other such commercial activities became part of his life. Their management agreement seems to have operated on no more than an initial handshake, though in latter years, at least, it was the savvy Shurley who was in charge of John's day-to-day diary. Clive and John shared a much-needed sense of the absurd, and had a down-to-earth opinion of musicians, their habits and demands – something that would come in useful in their next venture.

Dandelion Records was born of frustration – specifically, the frustration felt by Peel that a significant number of artists he liked simply didn't have record deals. He felt this meant they were unlikely to become as widely known as they deserved. So the object was not monetary gain, which was just as well, since Dandelion remained a stubbornly non-profitmaking venture, but more an attempt by both to put something back into the business they loved.

Taking Elektra as its tasteful template, 'Dandy' (as it was known) released its first record by folk singer Bridget St John in 1969, and would clock up some two dozen albums and around half as many singles during its brief, four-year life. Bridget met Peel through mutual friend Pete Roche who ran a folk/poetry combo, the Occasional Word Ensemble. John instantly fell in love with her music and invited her to perform on his *Night Ride* programme. 'To Be Without A Hitch'/'Autumn Lullaby' became one of two 45s to launch the label and resurfaced later on her debut LP. She was chosen for the launch because, Peel explained simply, 'She was a friend and I liked the stuff she did.' If ever a label was a labour of love, then Dandelion was surely it.

Ask Me No Questions was released a couple of months later as the first Dandelion album – its gatefold sleeve featured a baby Bridget being held by her grandma. Peel's minimal production values – the set was recorded in just ten hours over two evenings at CBS studios – wisely let her music speak for itself. She was aided and abetted by Simon Stable on bongos and guitarists Ric Sanders and John Martyn: as Bridget later observed, 'It's important to play with people who like what you do.' The record's sparseness only seemed to enhance its intimacy and purity, the pastoral splendour of the title track with the birds singing and church bell ringing (Peel's idea) capturing the gentle zeitgeist. A follow-up, *Songs For The Gentle Man*, appeared in the spring of 1971, but Bridget was never to achieve the potential Peel felt she had of being 'the second Sandy Denny'.

There were few unifying threads running through Dandelion's roster – except, of course, that all the acts featured enjoyed Peel's patronage. A notable early single was a re-cut of 'Be-Bop-A-Lula' by Gene Vincent, by then mere months from a premature death. A band from Derby, known as Coyne-Clague (and later Siren), released two albums for Dandelion. They were a great combo, mixing singer Kevin Coyne's predilection for primitive rock'n'roll with his more arty leanings, which resulted in thoughtful songs of 'hate and pain'. Yet their demo tape had come without an accompanying return address, so Peel resorted to pasting 'wanted' notices on lamp-posts, as one would for a missing cat. Perseverance paid off, though Richard Branson's fledgling Virgin label would enjoy the fruits of Coyne's solo career, not Dandelion.

Goodies comedian Bill Oddie produced an in-joke version of traditional Yorkshire folk song 'On Ilkla Moor Baht 'At', performed in the over-the-top style of Joe Cocker. Dandelion also hosted Mancunians Stackwaddy – punks before punk was invented, whose lead singer had been known to relieve himself from the stage. Amazingly the former building-site labourers had the chance to record a second album, which rejoiced in the title of *Bugger Off!*, apparently a retort to Peel when he made a rare suggestion as to musical arrangement.

The music that emerged with the Dandelion logo, from Siren to Stackwaddy and beyond, was every bit as distinctive as the label's emphatically non-corporate logo. Yet though the occasional superstar took an interest – Pink Floyd drummer Nick Mason produced a brace of long-players by the anarchic Principal Edwards Magic Theatre (who spent many of their off-stage hours squatting in John's flat, much to the long-suffering Sheila's annoyance), while Gene Vincent's one and only album featured members of the Byrds and Steppenwolf – the budget was never there to expose this quality music to a wider public. 'When you can't afford full-page ads in the music press,' Peel told *Record Collector* in 1994, 'artists become very resentful . . . there's no faster way of losing friends.' But the music had the opposite effect.

Peel's creative input had been in evidence when new signings The Way We Live changed their name to Tractor at his suggestion. It transpired he had got the idea while looking out of his kitchen window at his Suffolk home: 'I suppose we're lucky a muck-spreader or hearse wasn't going past,' joked guitarist Jim Milne who, with Steve Clayton (drums) formed the nucleus of an ever-shifting line-up that continued in sporadic fashion through to the present.

Medicine Head's 'Pictures In The Sky' finally took Dandelion into the Top Thirty in 1971. When aired two years earlier, the two-piece band's debut single, 'His Guiding Hand', had seen the Dandelion 'office' inundated by enquiries from the some of the biggest names in rock – Pete Townshend, Manfred Mann, Eric Clapton and ex-Yardbird Keith Relf (who eventually produced and even joined the band). Not bad for a 7-incher recorded in the band's kitchen and reputedly costing a mere 30 bob (£1.50) to make. On the subject of money, no advances were paid to Dandelion artists, but any profits were split fifty-fifty with the artist, the record company's share being ploughed back into the business.

Things looked promising for Dandelion. But in Clive Selwood's words, 'as it became successful so John lost interest,' and the story ended in 1972 by mutual consent. Ironically, one of that year's releases had been a sampler, *There Is Some Fun Going Forward*, the sleeve of which featured Peel (and nubile female friend) naked in a bath! Dandelion's spell as a functioning label – which encompassed distribution arrangements with, consecutively, CBS, Warner Bros and Polydor – had been as short as the plant from which it took its name. (In fact, Dandelion and Biscuit were the names of Peel's pet hamsters, suggested by his erstwhile flatmate Marc Bolan: Biscuit Music was the associated publishing company.)

Ultimately, Dandelion will be regarded as an A&R source for other labels: Medicine Head had further hits with Polydor, while singer-songwriters Bridget St John and Clifford T. Ward went to Chrysalis and Charisma respectively. But to those who followed its evolution Dandelion was rather more than that – an early indie whose spirit, suss and innate good taste would make it one of the most collectable labels in the years that followed as enthusiasts attempting to locate the strictly limited pressings paid ridiculous prices for them. Clive Selwood made the releases available again through See For Miles in the mid-1990s, but with that label's demise they are once again out of print.

Away from the twin challenges of radio broadcasting and running a record company, John's personal life had barely had time to stabilize after his split from first wife Shirley. As he revealed in 1969 to readers of a publication called *The Dee Jay Book*, the scars were still fresh. 'I am married, in actual fact,' he wrote, 'but my wife and I are separated. My wife and I were very young when we married and, I think, did so for all the wrong reasons.' He was, he said, 'surprised' that men still found it necessary to get married and concluded that since no children resulted from his first union: 'No one else has ever really been hurt by our parting.'

It would take quite some woman to turn around such a

philosophy, but Sheila Mary Gilhooly did just that. Described by Clive Selwood as 'a cheery, down-to-earth Yorkshire lady', and maintaining the Ravenscroft family's connections to the textiles industry as the daughter of a millworker, she was destined to suffer the ignominy of the nickname 'The Pig' in all Peel's writings about his private life. This referred to her snorting laugh rather than any physical characteristic, and was symbolized by a silver, pig-shaped ring he wore on his left hand.

The pair met in the late 1960s when Peel was making a foray into television on the show *How It Is*. Together with *Oz* magazine editor Richard Neville, Peel was apparently not averse to scanning the studio audience for likely conquests before filming commenced, and it was love at first sight. 'She was wearing dark green and she just looked so wonderful,' Peel has said. 'I thought, "I can't let her get away," and I devised a strategy for getting a note to her asking her to go out.' The feeling took time to be reciprocated – 'She agreed to it reluctantly, but I persuaded her' – and formed the basis of a relationship that was to last some three-and-a-half decades.

It had, John would later admit, been something of a shock to give up the bachelor lifestyle of a nationally known disc jockey. 'At the time, I was going out with a lot of different people . . . but most of them were models that didn't model, or actresses that didn't act, and they'd all sit around and I'd say stupid things. They'd say "Wow, man, that's really beautiful . . ." And Sheila would just say, "Ee, you're a daft bugger!" I used to think this was grotesquely disrespectful, but over a period of time it dawned on me that I was, indeed, a daft bugger, and she was absolutely right. So, over a period of time the models disappeared, and the actresses disappeared, and Sheila stayed . . .'

John and his schoolteacher love married on 31 August 1974 – 'The day after my birthday, so I'd not forget.' The reception took place in London's Regent's Park. John's sheepdog Woggle was present, while Rod Stewart took time out of his superstar schedule to be best man. The colour scheme was not just white but Liverpool red and white – Peel's resolutely pillarbox-hued suit is almost impossible to look at on film footage. The processional music was 'You'll Never Walk Alone' and Clive Selwood was, of course, an honoured guest. In short, an object lesson in how to combine the three cornerstones of your life.

Mr and Mrs Ravenscroft (as the marriage certificate had it) made their home in Suffolk at Peel Acres, a thatched cottage that set them back a shade over £10,000 in 1971. It was so named due to the fact that John once bought two acres of land adjoining the picturesque, L-shaped building as a birthday present for his beloved. It was a typically romantic gift: after Sheila had been involved in a minor road shunt, he filled the rear-ended Renault with flowers, admitting that, 'Sometimes I worry that I place too much emotional burden on her because she represents all women to me.' Maybe the most telling remark of all, though, was when he commented, 'She stops me feeling sorry for myself.'

The extra acreage came in handy, as a tennis court was eventually added, paid for by the proceeds of a voice-over for an Andrex toilet-paper commercial. Peel's laconic tones were in huge demand for such ventures, though sometimes he could be very choosy as to the type of projects to which he lent his vocal cords. Clive Selwood once negotiated a sky-high percentage for the B-side of a give-away single extolling the virtues of a financial institution. It seemed a done deal, given that his friends the Faces were to adorn the A-side of the promotional release. But when Peel discovered the identity of the bank, whose links with apartheid South Africa made them a despised name among the student fraternity with whom he was such a hit, he pulled out of the arrangement immediately.

Children arrived – in order of appearance from the mid-1970s, William Anfield, Alexandra Anfield, Thomas Dalglish and Florence Shankly. Florence's birth in the early 1980s was particularly traumatic, and John feared for Sheila's very life: 'She lost a lot of weight and was very ill indeed. She came to me about four o'clock one morning and said she thought that the baby was about to be born ... I went and made her a cup of tea and put on Rachmaninov's Second Piano Concerto and when it had finished we drove off to the hospital, both of us thinking separately that she was going to be very ill, possibly die. In the event she was all right, and Florence was born a most healthy and pugnacious child.' (Peel would later donate his voice-over talents to the Blood Transfusion service in gratitude.)

His children's names betrayed John's continuing love of Liverpool Football Club, even though he was now domiciled not across the river but in deepest East Anglia, where he was happy to enjoy 'D-list celebrity status ... being asked to open the local village fete, and that's it.' He and the Pig invested in season tickets at Portman Road, home of local team Ipswich Town, but his heart remained at Anfield.

According to John, his earliest football recollections came when he was packed off to prep school at the age of seven. 'At the first boarding school I went to, there were about eighty boys. Seventy-eight of them supported Manchester United, I supported Liverpool and there was one boy who wasn't interested in football.' While the experience of fighting his corner against such odds may have cemented his affection for Liverpool, it also ensured he would grow up with a dislike of Manchester United, or, as he himself said, 'My prejudice against United has been lifelong.'

His love affair with Liverpool FC was, of course, conducted from afar during the Dallas and West Coast years of the 1960s and, prior to global television and the internet, news would often be in short supply. There is a story, never confirmed but quite possibly true, that John only began to get homesick after Liverpool were crowned League champions for the seventh time in 1966. Certainly, by the start of the following year he was back in England and never left again.

While there will be many thousands who remember him purely on the strength of his pioneering radio show, countless others will recall with equal affection his almost constant championing of Liverpool Football Club. Called upon in the 1980s to be presenter of TV's *Top of the Pops*, John would leave the viewer with little doubt as to which team he supported; a female relative of the family knitted him a red jumper that simply stated 'League Champions' and then underneath listed each and every year the club had lifted the honour. A year later and John would have a new jumper, newly knitted and bearing testament to the latest success of the men from Anfield. It was a simple yet highly effective statement and very much typical of the man.

If Liverpool were the number-one love of his football life, perhaps Ipswich ran them close in later life. The Peels developed an affinity with the club over the years, and John was disappointed that he was unable to get to Wembley in 2000 for their play-off final against Barnsley owing to a long-standing charity commitment in Bury. He got home in time to watch the end of the match on television – and when Ipswich won, to make up for the disappointment of losing twelve months earlier, he rushed out and painted the scoreline – '4–2' – in big blue numbers on his wall.

He was known locally for his support of Liverpool, of course, and had one or two friendly run-ins with the local kids over the subject of football loyalties. 'I'd say, "What team do you support?" – "Manchester United" – and you say, "Here's a map of England, find me Manchester!" And they don't know where it is, but they support Manchester United. I say, "You only support them 'cause they win everything!"'

Though John had been able to enjoy the glory days of Liverpool FC during the 1970s and 1980s as the Merseyside club swept all before them, he also experienced a number of lows to go with the undoubted highs. Present on the night of the Heysel Stadium disaster in 1985, when fights between opposing fans resulted in loss of life, it was claimed afterwards that he developed a real fear of crowds after witnessing the scenes of chaos and carnage. The day after the Hillsborough disaster, four years later, John broke down and cried on air as the death toll continued to rise.

Even when the occasion demanded a little decorum and grace, John Peel could be relied upon to remind people of his allegiance. On collecting his 1993 Sony Award, he tearfully told the audience, 'This award just goes to show that radio is a wonderful medium for short, fat Liverpool supporters.'

In fact, football ran as a theme through John Peel's life in much the same way the word 'Blackpool' runs through a stick of rock. The Undertones may have been acknowledging this when they used a Subbuteo player on the cover to their single 'My Perfect Cousin' as well as to illustrate a lyric from the song, while another favourite of the post-punk era, Half Man Half Biscuit, managed to combine football and music with the legendary 'All I Want For Christmas Is A Dukla Prague Away Kit'.

As his children grew up, their middle names became a source of great embarrassment to them. But, as their unrepentant father pointed out, 'If I'd been a supporter of Shrewsbury Town they'd be called . . . well, William for example is called William Robert Anfield Ravenscroft, and if I'd been a Shrewsbury Town supporter he'd have been called William Robert Gay Meadow, which would have been difficult to live with.'

When talking of his family on *Desert Island Discs* in 1989, he confessed to feeling proud that Thomas, his younger son, bore a slight resemblance to former Liverpool great Kenny Dalglish: 'He's blond and stocky and quite good at football, and in fact scored his first hat-trick a couple of weeks ago.' Yet, as with his musical heroes, he seemed to keep a respectful distance from the sporting legends he idolized: when player/manager Dalglish once visited Radio One, Peel was too overawed to meet him – 'I'd just burst into tears,' he said. 'He's done so much for us.'

During the short period Trevor Dann produced *The John Peel Show* in 1983 he actually managed to engineer (no pun intended) a meeting with Dalglish. In January Radio One was broadcasting a week of programmes from the city where British rock and pop began, and persuaded Peel to return to his home city. A pilgrimage to Anfield was inevitable, but the Reds' unexpected 2–1 defeat at the hands of Brighton and Hove Albion in the fifth round of the FA Cup rather marred the occasion for the fanatical DJ. John was so depressed, in fact, that Dann's smuggling a Studer tape machine on to the terraces yielded few words suitable for broadcast. Neither did the meeting with Dalglish the following day – the DJ's upset at the shock Cup exit matched in enthusiasm by the footballer's professionally pat answers – 'So in the end *I* had to ask the questions and we dubbed in the commentary later,' Dann recalled.

One of the greatest occasions of Peel's life, running a close second to the birth of his children, came in Paris in 1981 when Alan Kennedy scored the winning goal against Real Madrid in the Parc des Princes to win the European Cup Final for Liverpool. 'That was probably as good a moment as I've ever had,' Peel beamed. The event had given him a rare chance, even more rarely taken up, to get close to one of his heroes – in this case former manager Bill Shankly, under whom the club had won League and Cup honours in the 1960s and early 1970s and who was an honoured member of the travelling party. 'He had a drink with Bill,' friend and Liverpool player Alan Hansen recalled, 'and Bill said, "Can you get my bag, there, John?" It was the ultimate for John Peel, to be taking Bill Shankly's bag, because he regarded him as a god.'

Hansen, who would become a BBC colleague of Peel's in the 1990s when he became a pundit on TV's *Match of the Day*, recalls days the pair 'would just sit and talk football, and he'd talk about Liverpool constantly – it was the only time I ever saw him animated.' A picture of Shankly adorned the kitchen wall at Peel Acres, alongside that of another legendary 'manager' . . . John Walters.

Peel rarely tried to use his celebrity to get 'freebies', though he told the story against himself of one time he did, for Liverpool against St Etienne. He had his secretary call the ground to try to get a ticket, but the line was a bad one. '"Hello, BBC, John Peel . . . Hello, John Peel from the BBC." In the end the girl on the other end just said: "Well, you can go and tell John Peel to fuck off." And I thought, "Great, that's exactly what *I* would have done."'

Scots footballer Pat Nevin, now retired, is a noted indie-music lover and held Peel in high regard. The pair became friends during the player's spell on Merseyside in Everton's colours, and he invited the Peels to the FA Cup Final of 1989 as his guests. It was a highly charged final, following hard on the heels of the Hillsborough disaster in which ninety-five Reds fans lost their lives (one more supporter died later). But, as Liverpool were playing local rivals Everton, the event was nothing short of a celebration of Merseyside football. And, as Nevin was playing for the Blues, his guests entered into the spirit of the occasion by sitting in among the opposition.

'If you're in the Cup Final you want your friends and family to be there,' Nevin remembered, 'and of course I asked John to come along with Sheila. I was playing for Everton, and John's a Liverpool fan, and of course in the middle of all the Everton fans John turned up with his red scarf for Liverpool. I wouldn't have expected anything else from him!'

Like many football fans, John was unhappy about the effect of satellite TV on the game. 'Football has been distorted by the application of television money,' he commented, 'because it means the rich get richer and the poor get poorer so it's very undemocratic.' That's a feeling Delia Smith would doubtless share. The owner of Ipswich's East Anglian rivals Norwich City, and a close neighbour of the Peels 'across the next field', was present when Liverpool last played Ipswich in the Premiership in the 1994–5 season. 'Sheila sat with the Ipswich supporters and John sat with the Liverpool supporters, and I just thought that was amazing . . . like they were true supporters of their teams.'

It was rare for our man to be lost for words when it came to the beautiful game. According to Alan Hansen, Peel possessed a great knowledge of football, 'and when you sit and listen to him he would be very, very passionate. I'm supposed to be an expert – but he's the expert and I'm the listener about what's happening at Liverpool, where it's going wrong, where it's going right. He would tell me what's happening in the football world.' Unfortunately, the converse was never true. 'I couldn't tell him what was happening in the music world. He said to me once, "What's your taste in music?" I said, "I love Billy Joel," and he went [shaking his head], "Can't see it, can't see it." I said, "Oh well, thanks very much!" I think he sold about 60 million records, but does that not count? Not to him it didn't. If he didn't like him, he didn't like him.'

Although he was a working DJ for more than forty years, it wasn't until 2002 that John Peel finally got to do a mix record, with *FabricLive.07* – recorded live at the Fabric Club in London. Even then, in among the reggae, drum'n'bass, techno and blues, was an intro that detailed Liverpool's many European Cup triumphs and the Kop Choir singing 'You'll Never Walk Alone'. Not surprisingly, that was a recording John Peel always said he wanted played at his funeral alongside the inevitable 'Teenage Kicks'.

As the subject of *Desert Island Discs* in 1989, John was asked – as are all subjects – to nominate a luxury item he'd take with him. His answer – a football – was revealing: 'I'd have to have a wall or something I could kick it against, but a football would give me a great deal of pleasure because ... as a boy playing football, I've always been a rather graceless creature, I don't dance, I've never danced, I've always been too inhibited to dance, [but] when I was playing football I always felt graceful. I feel as other people would feel when they were dancing, so a football would be essential.'

The man who couldn't dance and could only sing 'like a dolphin' was liberated with a ball at his feet ... or cheering on his heroes in red from the sidelines. At his fiftieth-birthday party, he lamented: 'Think my chances of making the Liverpool side are gone now. Might still be able to get a game at one of those London clubs, though.' Only John Peel could mix self-deprecation and Cockney-bashing to such deft effect.

When Paul Gambaccini paid tribute to his fellow veteran broadcaster in music-business journal *Music Week,* days after his death, he dug out a picture of John squatting, looking as uncomfortable as ever, as part of a 'team photo' of Radio One DJs. Not the famous Broadcasting House shot from 1967 this time, but on the turf of Wembley Stadium in 1979 when the station's presenters were let loose at half-time in a schoolboy international to take on a show business squad. 'I was, completely undeservedly, the first American to play at Wembley,' Gambo commented, 'but Peel scored a goal – and I have never seen a happier man.'

7

Punk and Disorderly

THERE'S A TEMPTATION to believe that John Peel's – and therefore the nation's – conversion to the punk cause came when he spun the Undertones' debut EP and was famously reduced to tears by the pure passion of 'Teenage Kicks'. As we've already learned, however, the Ramones were the group that worked the oracle in 1976, and it wouldn't be until September 1978 that the band from Northern Ireland, formed nearly three years earlier, made it to the airwaves in such spectacular fashion.

As with most things in life, the truth was less black-and-white than shades of grey. There was a definite period of transition between the old guard and the new. Take 29 September 1976, for example: '(I'm) Stranded' by Australian punks the Saints kicked off the show, but the rest of the broadcast was devoted to Stevie Wonder's extraordinary double album (plus bonus 7-inch disc) *Songs In The Key Of Life*. This was Peel at his most eclectic.

In some ways, punk was an obvious progression for Peel, given that the Sex Pistols came together in part due to guitarist Steve Jones and drummer Paul Cook's love of the Faces. Bob Harris was beaten up in the Speakeasy by an entourage associated with the Sex Pistols for being 'old regime', yet Peel mostly escaped such unwelcome attention.

For his former fans, though, the choice was stark: stay tuned or switch off. Many thousands were alienated by punk, and Peel felt the backlash. If the Ramones had the same effect on him as hearing Little Richard as a teenager – 'you felt rather threatened by it, it was so alien and terrifically exciting' – the flood of listeners who jammed the BBC switchboard were not calling to congratulate him: 'People phoned in and said, "You must never do this again" and then they wrote in afterwards and said, "You must never play any of these records ever again" . . . of course, I always find that very exciting!'

But the die was cast and, in the space of about a month, the average age of the audience dropped by about ten years. Much to Peel's delight, 'All those people who wanted to go on listening to Grateful Dead records for the rest of their lives obviously got off the train at that point.'

Peel found the short, sharp electric shock of songs such as 'Sheena Is A Punk Rocker' a refreshing counterpart to the fare he was listening to and playing five nights a week between the hours of 10 p.m. and midnight. It was a logical development, then, to discover and play music from other New York artists emerging at around the same time, such as Patti Smith and, later, Television. Yet there was another major discovery to come – aided by the fact that a related new musical movement was emerging just a few miles from Broadcasting House.

It was John Walters, not Peel himself, who took a stroll down Oxford Street in September 1976 to check out the 100 Club Punk Festival featuring, among others, the Sex

Pistols and the Clash. Walters later recalled being somewhat taken aback by the energy and menace generated by Johnny Rotten and therefore did not – to his eternal regret – offer the Pistols a Peel session there and then. But newly minted punk bands such as the Damned received invitations to the BBC's Maida Vale studio to lay down a session.

The Damned's first session, recorded that November and broadcast the following month, had been a source of worry to the production staff: would these young men enter Maida Vale's hallowed portals and start spitting at each other – or, even worse, at them? As it transpired, the five numbers attempted, including the first nationally distributed punk single 'New Rose', were recorded more or less live in the time it would take some bands to complete a couple of overdubs. Producer Jeff Griffin considered the Damned 'four of the nicest blokes I've ever worked with', and drummer Rat Scabies's mum even wrote in after the songs were aired to thank Peel for 'helping Christopher with his career'! (Prior to punk, Scabies's given name had been Chris Miller.)

The BBC hierarchy had been alerted to the punk movement, as were the tabloids, after an infamous interview on Thames TV's *Today* show, during which presenter Bill Grundy goaded the Sex Pistols (in particular Steve Jones) into swearing their heads off – in a teatime slot. Indeed, Ken Garner's *In Session Tonight* reveals that Radio One controller Derek Chinnery called John Walters on 6 December, less than a week after the onscreen swearfest, to request an assurance that Peel's show wouldn't be offering these characters a platform. The answer, 'We already have,' was not quite what he'd been hoping to hear.

Though absent from daytime radio, incendiary Sex Pistols singles such as 'Anarchy In The UK' (first aired by Peel on 19 November 1976), 'Pretty Vacant' and early Clash recordings became staples of Peel shows. Even today, old punks fondly recall the thrill of illicit pleasure the night Peel played the entire *Never Mind The Bollocks* album a few days before it was officially released in May 1977. With typical flair, he reserved the Pistols' 'God Save The Queen' single – still serving a touchline ban on radio airwaves – for the three minutes approaching midnight.

The Clash should, by rights, have taken their appointed place between John Cooper Clarke and the Climax Chicago Blues Band in the roll-call of legendary Peel sessions – but it never happened. Not that this was for want of trying: in fact, they started a session but decided halfway through that the equipment they were using wasn't up to the expected standard and so they declined to complete it. Needless to say, Peel, who considered such an attitude 'unbearably pretentious', especially for a so-called punk band, never forgot the slight. He'd even given Joe Strummer his first pre-fame exposure on the national airwaves when playing his band the 101ers' 'Keys To Your Heart', a fact that must have made this knockback all the stranger, though he continued to play Clash records.

Irish rockers Thin Lizzy seemed to survive the punk 'cull', largely one suspects due to their aggressive attitude: indeed, Phil Lynott would later collaborate with members of the Sex Pistols and perform as the Greedy Bastards. And when Nick Lowe, formerly bass player and vocalist with pub-rockers Brinsley Schwarz (who taped four Peel sessions between 1970 and 1975) came up with a Lizzy soundalike single in 'So It Goes', the first release by the new Stiff Records label, John liked it so much he played it every night of a late-August '76 week.

The radical changes in Peel's listening and playing habits were best reflected in his 'Festive Fifties', in which he would dedicate an entire show to playing his listeners' favourite tracks at Christmas. In December 1976 the battlements of the castle were still manned by the old guard, and such names as Led Zeppelin, Pink Floyd, Jimi Hendrix, Bob Dylan, Genesis and Free were enjoying a last hurrah. By the following festive season, however, there had been a total sea change. Although complications regarding the birth of his first daughter saw no fifty-song festive show, a list of Peel favourites at this time included the Clash's 'Complete Control', the Sex Pistols' 'Holidays In The Sun', the Rezillos' 'Can't Stand My Baby', the Motors' 'Dancing The Night Away' and even Althea and Donna's 'Uptown Top Ranking' – the latter betraying the DJ's growing fascination with reggae and dub.

Nightly playlists from this period were a perfumed garden of delights. Tracks veered from Prince Far I to X-Ray Spex via Eddie and the Hot Rods, Devo to Blondie then to a new Buzzcocks single, and then perhaps 'Venus' from Television's debut album. Peel's self-effacing presentation style remained the same, although this uncompromising new music alienated his previous audience who had grown accustomed to Little Feat and Pink Floyd and couldn't see that the Stranglers had anything in common with the Doors apart from a nifty keyboard player.

But for every pair of ears that turned away, another ten – belonging to teenagers across the country – pricked up. They tuned their transistor dials to Radio One late at night to hear music from new bands they were reading about in the music press, or whom they had perhaps never heard of at all. On any given night, Peel might drop the needle on the Damned, the Stranglers, Wire, Alternative TV, Subway Sect, the Jam, Elvis Costello, 999, Generation X, Ian Dury and the Blockheads, the Skids, the Vibrators, Magazine, the Saints, Penetration, Stiff Little Fingers, the Buzzcocks and sundry other extravagantly named outfits.

New listeners would naturally then take the next logical step of going out and buying these singles and albums – if they could find them, that is. The relationship between the Sex Pistols and the established music business was very much symptomatic of the problem: EMI had signed the band in October 1976, then ditched them one single later the following January after several bouts of bad publicity orchestrated by manager Malcolm McLaren. A&M Records picked up the Pistols, only to cut them loose within a week amid a storm of disapproval from their artist roster. Richard Branson then signed them to his independent Virgin label, but such problems made established record companies initially unwilling to handle any band with a hint of controversy attached to them.

This situation made Peel sessions even more crucial. With official releases slow to catch up with demand, and availability of indie releases patchy at best, Peel and Walters were generous in awarding sessions to bands that tickled their fancy whether they had a record contract or not. Siouxsie and the Banshees were given their first break through the medium of a Peel session. 'He gave us our chance to discover what it was like to be in a studio with those early sessions,' Siouxsie stated days after his death, adding, 'I know for a fact that those sessions were instrumental in getting us signed and releasing "Hong Kong Garden" as our first single in 1978.'

Unsigned acts who had sent in demo tapes, or who had little more than an independently released single or EP to their name, would be offered the opportunity to broadcast to bedrooms and living rooms across the nation. A small sample of bands that unpacked instruments and got down to business between 1976 and 1980 now reads like a mouthwatering selection of great or cult artists. This included the Only Ones, Magazine, the UK Subs, Ultravox! (with John Foxx, not Midge

Ure), the Mekons, the Adverts, X-Ray Spex, the Cure and Wire who – true to their artistic ideals – once abandoned punk principles completely and recorded one twelve-minute track.

Many bands recorded two or three sessions in quick succession and, well before the Strange Fruit label began to reissue these recordings, fans were feverishly taping and bootlegging the sessions and flogging them at markets or at gigs around the country. Where else could you hear Adam and the Ants' material outside their Marquee Club residency before they finally signed a deal? How many Sex Pistols fans tuned into John Lydon's Public Image Limited session in December 1979 to see what new musical clothes the emperor was wearing? How many discovered Can (a major PIL influence) on the back of that session?

Of course, for every band that went on to enjoy chart success or built a successful career there were several more who simply reflected the energy of their times. Quirky punks Spizz Oil (later known as Spizz Energi) got into the studio for the first time on the strength of supporting Siouxsie and the Banshees on tour. Their session was so much fun that they were swiftly signed up by Geoff Travis's Rough Trade label to record their first single. Without Peel, then, the world could conceivably have been deprived of the pleasure of hearing their punk classic 'Where's Captain Kirk?'

Although Peel warmly embraced punk, it was the subsequent new wave that really received the blowtorch of his enthusiastic patronage. By 1978, buzz-saw guitars and anti-establishment lyrics had become the stock in trade of punk bands such as the UK Subs, Sham 69 and the Angelic Upstarts – all of whom had their hearts in the right place – and accrued some chart success, but quickly began to sound musically fettered. Yet a multitude of other bands from Brighton to Scotland now began to create diverse fascinating music, drawing inspiration from all points of the compass. Simple Minds had an air of Roxy Music about them, the Gang of Four brought their jagged guitars and razor-sharp lyrical acuity to bear on a number of unorthodox subjects, while Liverpool's Echo and the Bunnymen allied a scally swagger to their Scouse wit. Then there were electronic experimentalists such as Sheffield's Cabaret Voltaire, the Human League and, of course, Gary Numan, whose Tubeway Army had featured on *The John Peel Show* some time before hitting the top of the charts with 'Are "Friends" Electric?'

As the major labels struggled to realign themselves with the new musical climate, small independent record labels such as Rough Trade, Stiff, Beggars Banquet, Mute, Industrial, Fast, Factory, Fetish, Cherry Red and Zoo began to push out great records. Bands also took ownership into their own hands and would self-finance a debut single or EP knowing that, if they sent their vinyl statements to Peel, he would listen to them and, if he liked them enough, play them. Famously, when it came to the Undertones' 'Teenage Kicks', Peel even announced on air that he had liked it so much that he was going to play it again, and promptly did so.

Peel was equally smitten by the magnificent clatter and pungent lyrics of Mark E. Smith's Fall and, after their debut session in May 1978, they ended up recording an unprecedented seventeen Peel sessions. They would also play at his fiftieth-birthday party, typically presenting a set of songs no one had heard before. 'Things like the Sex Pistols don't seem to have stood the test of time,' John was moved to remark, 'but if you listen to the first records by the Fall they sound as good as they ever did. That's unusual in any area of popular music.'

As so often, the connection had originally been made by John Walters, who first saw the Fall supporting Peel faves Siouxsie and the Banshees at Croydon. 'Danny Baker recommended I catch your performance,' he wrote to Smith, adding a note to his partner, 'The band seems to have the kind of defiant non-musical approach which ought to be encouraged.' (Baker, later to line up alongside Peel as a Radio One DJ, had emerged as a scribe for punk journal *Sniffin' Glue*.)

Sure enough, the Fall continue their idiosyncratic musical journey today, and it's odds-on that the majority of their loyal fan base first encountered them via John Peel. Indeed, despite the occasional minor hit single with late-1980s cover versions of songs by R. Dean Taylor ('There's A Ghost In My House') and the Kinks ('Victoria'), their career has been conspicuous by an almost total absence from the non-Peel airwaves.

The Fall's first recordings had actually been two cuts on a punk cash-in album, Virgin's *Short Circuit – Live At The Electric Circus*, recorded in their native Manchester, which featured two more future Peel favourites in the Buzzcocks and Joy Division, the latter known as Warsaw at the time. Renamed courtesy of a Nazi-concentration-camp novel, Joy Division recorded two sessions for Radio One's most sought-after show before their critically lauded debut album *Unknown Pleasures* came out in 1979.

Peel broke the news of the suicide of their lead singer the following May as if he had lost a close family friend: 'Bad news, lads. Ian Curtis from Joy Division has just died.' In the Festive Fifty of that year 'Atmosphere', 'Love Will Tear Us Apart' and 'Transmission' all made the Top Ten. And when Peel compiled his Millennium Fifty in 2000, 'Atmosphere' was number one with the Undertones' 'Teenage Kicks' at two.

Crucially, in the aftermath of Curtis's death, Peel was quick to give New Order a session, revealing to Joy Division fans that – like post-Syd Barrett Floyd – the remaining members retained a musical alchemy and spark that spawned a career which, like the Fall's, continues today. After Peel's death, bassist Pete Hook recalled that a long time elapsed before the band met the DJ who championed them: 'We were so nervous we had to have a couple of drinks. He was nervous about meeting us, too, which flabbergasted us.'

Peel's shyness was one reason it took him until the next decade to grace *Top of the Pops* as a regular presenter, despite many of his favourite bands making it to the screen. Artists who did sessions for his show expected to turn up at Maida Vale to find Peel waiting to greet them. However, as a fan himself, Peel was as much in awe of bands as they were in awe of him, and when he did see them it was usually as an anonymous observer at concerts.

In many respects this was a good policy. Not only did it spare awkward introductions and handshakes but it allowed musicians to get on with the business at hand. Today Peel sessions hold pride of place in the discography of hundreds of bands. Indeed, when recording their debut album, goth-rock spearheads Bauhaus spent ages trying to recapture the exact sound and feel of the track 'Double Dare', recorded on their first Peel session in December 1979 and broadcast a month later. As it turned out, they found they could not replicate that musical energy, and simply applied for permission to use the Peel version instead.

The years between 1976 and 1980 were a musical golden age, the rollercoaster changes in the English scene throwing up all manner of movements. The Mod revival, power-pop and ska were just some of the variations. It was Peel, for instance, who introduced listeners to the Human League's early electronic pulsebeats, a fact little remembered when the band hit the top in late 1981 with the rather more accessible 'Don't You Want Me?' Of course, he also played Jerry and the Holograms, whose fame lasted no more than the three minutes it took to play the song. But that was the glory of *The John Peel Show*. It did not matter if the record charted, was on a major label or had Eric Clapton playing the accordion. If Peel liked it he played it – even if an Adam and the Ants version of the Village People's 'YMCA', with additional self-glorifying lyrics, left him short of words and in a state of bemused amusement.

Needless to say, Peel's association with the Ants, who went on to become a chart-topping panto-pop act in their New Romantic incarnation, extended only as far as their struggling years: the three sessions spanned some fourteen months from January 1978. 'The late 1970s was the only time the programme was fashionable,' he'd later squirm, 'and I didn't really like the experience. I felt rather as I imagine bands must feel when they become fashionable, that the audience expect certain things of them which they might not necessarily want to go on doing.' By the time of the release of 'Prince Charming' in September 1981, he'd turned his attention elsewhere. The Ants no longer needed his help.

One welcome by-product of the new-wave revolution was the increase in female singers and musicians. While 1960s women had by and large been out-front decorative 'dolly birds' such as Sandie Shaw, comparatively few had been seen wielding guitars – especially electric ones. But the new world order saw the likes of Gaye Advert (Adverts, bass), Lora Logic (X-Ray Spex, saxophone), and later Chrissie Hynde (Pretenders, guitar) make a mark on their various instruments – and there were many more. Even frontwomen like Siouxsie Sioux and Poly Styrene were now competing on something approaching their own terms.

But the Slits, who John claims recorded his two favourite Peel sessions ever, were something else again. Four young women with no musical training, a singer known as Ari Up who was just fourteen, a drummer called Palmolive and a surfeit of attitude, they could never have hoped to have graced a stage except then and there. Yet in terms of influencing other females to make music, they were rivalled at the time only by America's Runaways, featuring Joan Jett.

By this time, Peel had shifted his weekly column from *Disc & Music Echo* to *Sounds*, and it was in the latter that he confessed in March 1977 to having a 'heavy heart' due to the fact he'd yet to encounter the feisty female four-piece in concert. And so it was that Peel broke an unwritten rule in August when he ventured down to punk club the Vortex in Soho's Wardour Street to meet the girls: such was his fame that he could rarely turn up openly to gigs without being inundated with demo tapes and unwanted attention.

Fortunately, the Vortex's late show times meant Peel could saunter down Oxford Street once he'd finished his broadcast, and he was not disappointed with what he saw and heard. In any case, the fact the band had taken tabloid flak for their upfront name would probably have been enough in itself to encourage a booking. John Walters felt it was the duty of the BBC to record them 'for posterity'. The results, broadcast in September 1977 and May 1978, certainly, in Peel's words, 'summed up the spirit of the era', and would have done so even more had the engineers, both of whom were guitarists, not insisted on tuning up the girls' instruments between songs – a luxury not permitted in live performance. (A third Peel session without drummer Palmolive is listed for late 1981 in *In Session Tonight*, but by then their moment had passed.)

The Undertones would be worthy of a major footnote in music history, if only for the fact that they produced John Peel's favourite record ever. Yet the way they and Peel first hooked up is a story in itself; the fact they hailed from Northern Ireland and were unable to approach the

London-based music business is another. It was their geographical distance from Maida Vale that led to an early demonstration of Peel's keenness to assist: with air tickets beyond his show's budget, he agreed to fund a session out of his own pocket. Guilt over the fact that he had sat on their demo tape for some two months, such was the quantity of music he was receiving, may have had something to do with this – but he certainly made up for it, as lead guitarist Damian O'Neill recalls:

'He wrote a really nice letter: "Dear Undertones, I've behaved like a typical music business arsehole over your tape, and I'm genuinely sorry about this. Really liked the tape. I think you should record a session for us. I can't afford [for] you to come over to London to do a session, but I'd like to actually pay for it myself for you to do it in Northern Ireland if you can." It was incredible for somebody like John Peel to do that, to dip into his own pocket. So consequently we did the four songs and he did broadcast it within a couple of weeks.'

Ironically, neither this nor the four subsequent sessions they did for Peel contained 'Teenage Kicks' – maybe it was pointless trying to challenge perfection. Asked many years later why the track continued to hold a prime place in his affections, John admitted he'd yet to come up with a satisfactory answer. 'There's nothing you could add to it or subtract from it that would improve it, that's the best I can do . . . Maybe once a fortnight, after a few days of listening to sizzling new releases and worrying that the music is merging into a characterless soup, I play "Teenage Kicks" to remind myself exactly how a great record should sound.'

Such was Peel's attachment to the Undertones that hearing them played on the radio by another DJ produced an emotional reaction that surprised even him. 'I was driving up to see Liverpool play and was in a traffic jam round Stoke-on-Trent,' he recalled, 'and I heard Peter Powell play "Teenage Kicks", which I'd been playing for months. To hear it played by someone else was a stupendous thing and I actually burst into floods of tears in the traffic jam . . . I still can't play "Teenage Kicks" without segueing another track in afterwards to give myself time to regain composure.'

Singer Feargal Sharkey who, after quitting the Undertones for a brief solo career, has remained in the business – appropriately on the radio side of music – paid simple tribute in the *New Musical Express* on Peel's death: 'When he played "Teenage Kicks", it literally changed my life,' he stated. The singer also revealed that it had been Sheila sticking her head round the door at Peel Acres and saying, 'That's the best thing you've played all day' that pushed Peel into putting it on his show that night. Of such things are careers made, not to mention underlining his importance as the nation's tastemaker.

Other than the Undertones, late 1978 would be most notable for the debut Peel session by long-time friends and favourites the Cure. Hailing from Crawley, a sprawling town languishing under the flight path of Gatwick Airport, they were confederates of Siouxsie and the Banshees – indeed, guitarist and Cure head honcho Robert Smith would do double duty, playing for both bands on tour, when two Banshees, including six-stringer John McKay, quit on the eve of departure. But the band would soon graduate from support status to headlining in their own right, with help from Peel who gave the Cure a session a year from 1978 to 1982.

While 2-Tone, the multi-racial ska-based music that emanated from Coventry, is regarded as a 1980s phenomenon, it's worth noting that no fewer than four of its leading lights – the Specials, the Selecter, the Beat and

Madness – all cut their first Peel sessions in 1979. He was particularly taken by the Specials, the group led by Jerry Dammers whose record label named the phenomenon, to the extent that he played their May 1979 session four times over the course of the summer. This, of course, conferred great prestige and credibility on the band, who by September had a Top Ten single on 2-Tone and a label distribution deal with Chrysalis.

Another major musical movement to receive Peel's assistance was the explosion of Merseyside bands led by the previously mentioned Echo and the Bunnymen, whose lead singer Ian McCulloch shared John's fanaticism for all things Liverpool FC-related. Peel gave an early play to Orchestral Manoeuvres in the Dark's debut single 'Electricity' (the duo hailed from the other side of the Mersey) while fellow Liverpudlians the Teardrop Explodes, featuring notable eccentric and long-time Peel aficionado Julian Cope, and Pink Military, also received their first national radio exposure on *The John Peel Show* in 1979.

Fame and fortune, at least on a limited scale, might well attend those fortunate enough to be invited to record a Peel session. Yet the man himself, by no means an attention-seeker, had understandable reservations about this. Take, for example, the case of the Ruts, a punk band from West London. The band released their first single, 'In A Rut', on People Unite, the label of Peel's favourite reggae band, Misty In Roots – a reflection of the close affinity between punk and reggae. The coverage this January 1979 session received, and the promise shown by the track 'Babylon's Burning' – a future hit single – led directly to a contract offer from Virgin Records. 'They then started making money and having successful records,' Peel told *New Musical Express* a decade later, 'and [vocalist] Malcolm Owen got into heroin and died. And you sometimes think, if you *hadn't* played the record, if Virgin *hadn't* signed them, would he have had a brief but frustrating career and ended up as a brickie but alive? But then, if you thought about those things, you'd never do *anything* . . .'

Another soon-to-be famous name to join the Peel backroom team in the late 1970s was future Radio One demi-supremo Trevor Dann, who began producing Peel sessions in 1979. But John Walters, as ever, was still calling the shots, and it was in this very year that he made what he calls his 'second big mistake'. The first was not obtaining the Sex Pistols' services; the second was to grant the Police a session. John Peel himself has denied it ever happened (most notably on *Desert Island Discs*, where he bracketed them with fellow 'outcasts' U2 and Dire Straits), but the bible *In Session Tonight* tells, in plain black and white, of four songs recorded and broadcast in July 1979.

The Police were two ex-name musicians (Andy Summers from Soft Machine and the New Animals, Stewart Copeland from Curved Air) and a jazz-loving bass player (Sting) with newly bleached blond hair who surfed the new wave to success. They saw their chance and took it, so good luck to them – but for Peel it must have smacked of the early 1970s years he'd hated so much, when any new group seemed to feature at least one member of a formerly famous ensemble.

Walters had, in fact, mentally turned the Police down after seeing them play a London pub venue, but Peel's exposure to them on a Dutch festival date when they played 'particularly well' swayed the boss man. Yet there's little doubt they ran counter not only to punk's philosophy, but to all that the Peel show held dear. Simple Minds, another band of the era to rub off their rough edges and achieve superstardom in the 1980s, also made their Peel session debut around this time. Thus with the exception of the arrival of the Psychedelic Furs on the scene, what had been an epochal decade both for music and John Peel ended with something of a whimper – admittedly, after a series of explosive bangs.

Peel himself had seen many changes in the 1970s: he was now a married man with children and had carved out a domestic idyll for himself away from the hustle and bustle of London life. The challenge of filling five nights a week with good music had been met, and the Peel session 'brand' well and truly established. In retrospect, it's amazing that what had started out as a piece of typical BBC economy, to save on 'needle time', had become an unique way of not only preserving but creating musical history.

Looking back on the era for the benefit of *Peeling Back The Years* – a series of six shows broadcast on Radio One in 1987 – Peel would deny there'd been any grand plan: 'I don't pursue particular movements . . . the punk thing dominated as it did only because there wasn't anything else interesting at the time, or at least that interested me. But after the first careless rapture of that had diminished, I went back to the way I'd been before, looking around at various areas of music and trying to find what I regarded as the best in those different areas – rock, folk, reggae . . .'

The restoration of variety into the programme, challenging his own and his listeners' assumptions, was clearly key. 'In a way,' he agreed, 'I was happier than I had been during punk itself, when I was beginning to feel as though I was being compromised by the requirements and expectations of the people who listened to the programme.'

Nevertheless, in many respects, it was the evangelistic work Peel carried out during this period that would ensure his continued employment by Radio One. So many of the bands and artists he championed at the time, who went on to become some of the brightest stars of the rock firmament, would have raised merry hell had there been any intimation that his reign was threatened.

While the coming months would see Walters on the way to becoming a radio star in his own right, the 'dream team' would survive another decade before being consigned to history. But when it comes to making history, no period of John Peel's radio show would eclipse the late 1970s in terms of excitement, as anyone who lived and listened through it will confirm.

8

From Hip-hop
to Hardcore

As the decade that taste forgot gave way to the era of style over substance, *The John Peel Show* was itself moving into new territory. A frenzy of home-grown, guitar-driven punk had dominated during the previous two years or so, but many newer bands had put their own distinctive twist on the formula, exemplified by the clutch of Liverpool bands headed by Echo and the Bunnymen and the Teardrop Explodes, Mod revivalists such as Secret Affair and the Chords, and the emerging 2-Tone movement.

Peel was in his element, as he revealed in *Peeling Back The Years* in 1987: 'I've never, as far as I can recall, thought about what was going to happen next, because I was too much enmeshed in what was going on now. I like these things to come as a surprise. Like when the 2-Tone thing came along – if someone had told me at the beginning of that year that I'd be scouring the second-hand record shops for old ska and bluebeat records, I'd have thought they were nuts. But that's what I was doing, and I kind of like the element of surprise ...'

To give some idea of the sheer variety of sounds to be heard at this time, January 1980 alone saw debut Peel sessions by UB40, Simple Minds and Bauhaus, and as the year progressed these debutants were joined by the Birthday Party (Nick Cave's first group, recorded in September), Altered Images and Orange Juice (both October). These last two were the precursors of a wave of Scottish bands to emerge during late 1980 and early '81, with the Fire Engines, Josef K and the Associates following hard on their heels. Of these, Altered Images were the first Peel encountered, and he later recalled that the experience had a profound effect on him: 'I first heard them on a demo tape. Actually, I could take you to the exact spot on the road, it affected me that strongly . . . It was one of those occasions when I was in the car, shovelling demo tape after demo tape into the player, taking them out again and throwing them across the car with foul oaths; all rather a dangerous thing to do, really. But "Dead Pop Stars" came through the speakers, and I got home and phoned John [Walters] and said, "We must book these people as soon as we can."' (Perhaps it was the ultimate tribute to Peel that singer Clare Grogan should later forge a post-performing career in music television presentation.)

Alongside such up-to-the-minute delights, John's audience might also find themselves listening to 1960s crooner Roy Orbison, surf-guitar pioneer Dick Dale or a spot of dub reggae, a wildly eclectic mix that typified the man's approach to his art and which you could hear nowhere else. On pirate Radio London he'd rewritten the rulebook, refusing to run adverts and news bulletins during his broadcasts, and throughout his time at Radio One he'd never been afraid to introduce new concepts, weathering a deluge of abuse from his less adventurous listeners when he'd dared to play early reggae records or aired the first punk sessions. In essence, John

Peel was playing to an audience made in his own image, constantly keeping in mind the sort of radio programme he most wanted to hear. In a 1989 interview, he explained it thus: 'I like the idea of people driving along, listening to the radio and going "*What the hell is that?*" and turning it up.'

Despite his maverick tendencies, and despite rumours to the contrary that surfaced periodically throughout his career, Peel's position at Radio One was never under serious threat. Radio critic Gillian Reynolds probably hit the nail on the head when she offered this view in the 1999 television special to mark his sixtieth birthday: 'The BBC had always regarded John with interest, bemusement, tolerance, even . . . simply because he was posh. It was always borne in mind that he went to a public school . . . and that he came from a well-off family from the Wirral, so they always knew that he wasn't really one of those motormouth louts, he was really someone to be taken quite seriously. I think they also realized that there was a sense in which he was their credibility, for an awfully long time.'

The man himself later gave a slightly different explanation: 'Once they realize you do what you do reasonably well, and there are people who want to hear it, they leave you to get on with it. People never quite believe this, but at no time in all the years I've been on Radio One has anyone in the management told me what I should and shouldn't be playing.'

As 1980 drew to a close, a small group of experimental bands found themselves the subject of interest from the Peel camp. Cabaret Voltaire, who had formed in Sheffield some six years earlier, were marked out alongside the Leather Nun, Throbbing Gristle and Clock DVA as the leading lights in a new musical genre dubbed 'industrial'. It was just the sort of thing Peel loved – bleak, menacing soundscapes that challenged preconceptions and acted as an antidote to any complacency that might be creeping up on this seasoned DJ. (His Krautrock favourites Neu! from the early 1970s had a similar effect on the man.)

In retrospect, the period that followed was something of an anticlimax. The burst of energy that punk had injected into the music scene had been sufficient to carry through into the new decade, but it wasn't long before its commercial potential was exhausted and more demanding music was once again consigned to the periphery. In a move symptomatic of the times, the immensely influential Hüsker Dü were dropped by major label Warners, victims of an industry increasingly interested only in commercial success.

Anyone looking for something out of the ordinary had to dig deeper for it and, as the decade wore on, John Peel's show was virtually the only place in the British media where cutting-edge rock and avant-garde experimentation could find a voice. It's no exaggeration to say that Peel gave vital early exposure to almost all of the significant artists to emerge during the period.

First to benefit in 1981 were New Order, whose debut session was recorded in January and broadcast the following month. It included four songs, all later featured on the band's debut LP *Movement*, and was an important early opportunity to hear what was to become one of the decade's most influential bands.

In June, the Chameleons – another Mancunian band whose work has subsequently grown in stature – also got their initial exposure through a Peel session. And in November, four gawky kids from Sheffield took their first step on the road to fame. It would be a long hard slog, but Pulp's debut session way back at the start of the 1980s marked the beginning of a road that culminated in their triumphant appearance on the main stage at Glastonbury in 1995, although by then only singer Jarvis Cocker remained from the 1981 line-up.

Like so many bands, Pulp's initial exposure was down to Peel's openness and commitment to new music. Jarvis Cocker explained how it had come about: 'When we eventually got round to having some songs that were able to be listened to by other people, we'd just gone and recorded them, and then we found out that Peel was doing a roadshow at the Polytechnic in Sheffield. I went down with these tapes, with hand-drawn covers and stuff, and hung around nervously 'til he'd finished, then jumped in front of him with the cassette. He said, "Oh, I'll listen to that in the car on the way home," and I thought, "I wonder if that's true, I wonder if it'll go in the bin." Then about four days later, I got a call from John Walters wanting us to do a session on the show – that was amazing for us, 'cause we'd only done about three or four concerts; we were too young to go in pubs.'

Nevertheless, the early 1980s were largely devoid of any real excitement, with a series of mostly forgettable pop-oriented synthesizer bands relieved only occasionally by the more demanding work offered by the industrial contingent or the new wave of American noise merchants such as Bad Brains, Black Flag and the Circle Jerks. On the UK front, a similarly aggressive musical approach gave rise to a number of skinhead bands, a movement of limited musical endeavour swiftly dubbed 'Oi!' For all the sound and fury generated by the Oi! bands, and the controversy that surrounded the movement after a gig by the 4-Skins at Southall in July 1981 that ended in a pitched battle and a burned-out pub, music's ability to threaten the status quo seemed to have diminished.

It's probably fair to say that the Specials' 'Ghost Town', which seemed to capture the mood of the country during 1981's inner-city riots in Brixton and Toxteth, was one of the last significant political releases of the decade to reach the mainstream. It was left to Peel, through his support for the likes of Billy Bragg, McCarthy and the Great Leap Forward, to ensure that the anti-establishment message could still be heard in the years that followed.

During this period, Peel also made appearances as a presenter on *Top of the Pops* alongside the likes of Janice Long and David Jensen. Artistically, perhaps, this was not his finest hour, but he clearly relished the opportunity to bring a dash of English eccentricity to the proceedings, dressing in a variety of ridiculous costumes and announcing artists with his customary dry wit. A typical example came when Survivor appeared on the show to perform 'Eye Of The Tiger' in the summer of 1982, after which he memorably described them as 'the best band of that name in the world!' On another occasion, following a performance of the George Michael and Aretha Franklin duet 'I Knew You Were Waiting (For Me)', he is said to have quipped, 'They say Aretha can make any old rubbish sound good – and I think she just has!'

Peel's first experience of the *Top of the Pops* phenomenon had, in fact, come as far back as 1968, when an inability to remember the name of Amen Corner, the act he was presenting, led to a creditable impression of an open-mouthed goldfish. 'This officious person then walked up to me,' he later remembered, 'and in true Hollywood style muttered something like "I'll make sure you never work in television again." Which, at the time, all things considered, I reckoned not to be such a bad thing. I thought, "Right, that's fine, as long as you can guarantee it!"'

The difference now, he told Steve Blacknell, author of *The Story of Top of the Pops*, was that 'I don't have to pretend I'm twenty-two years old any more and jump up and down like a Butlin's redcoat saying things like "WHAT A SENSATION!" I just stand there and make fun of it – the producer likes it, and the bands do too, even bands like Bucks Fizz who you'd think would be a little serious and resentful.'

Off screen, 1982 was not a vintage year, although it did see the emergence of a genre whose longevity could never have been envisaged at the time. The phenomenon of rap had started at the end of the 1970s on the streets of New York and had attracted only limited interest until now, but listeners to Peel's shows were among the first in the UK to gain exposure to the likes of Grandmaster Flash, Kurtis Blow and the Sugarhill Gang, already veterans of the scene.

At the opposite end of the musical spectrum, although no less politically motivated, his old Soft Machine friend Robert Wyatt's exquisite rendition of Elvis Costello's 'Shipbuilding', a poignant anti-war song released at the time of the Falklands War, provided a sharp contrast to the gung-ho patriotism whipped up by the conflict, and many of the tracks from Wyatt's two 1982 albums, *Nothing Can Stop Us* and *Old Rottenhat* were aired throughout the year and into the next. Peel also featured Crass's barbed anti-war opus, the bitterly vitriolic 'How Does It Feel To Be The Mother Of 1,000 Dead?'

Out of left-field came tracks from Afrika Bambaataa's electro-funk masterclass *Planet Rock*, and a fifth Peel session in January from the Cure, who would reinvent themselves as purveyors of slightly skewed pop over the twelve months that followed. July saw the transmission of the debut session from perennial John Peel favourites the Cocteau Twins, who were genuinely unlike anything that had gone before. Liz Fraser's distinctive vocal stylings echoed across lush, often epic soundscapes to create a world in which time seemed to stand still. Their label, 4AD, became one of the most influential indie imprints of the 1980s, featuring a roster that, at various times, included Bauhaus, This Mortal Coil, the Birthday Party,

Colour Box, Xmal Deutschland, Xymox, Dead Can Dance, Throwing Muses and the Pixies, all of whom would feature prominently on Peel playlists as the decade progressed.

As with Altered Images' Clare Grogan a couple of years earlier, it was the quality of Liz Fraser's voice that attracted John Peel to the Cocteaus, a band that drew comparisons with Siouxsie and the Banshees in their early days. 'That always struck me as a nonsense, frankly,' he reflected. 'It was a fact that [Liz and Siouxsie] were two women singers with fairly strong and identifiable voices, but that didn't make the Cocteau Twins some kind of Siouxsie and the Banshees clones by any means. The big attraction for me was that extraordinary voice. I liked the sound of her voice in the same way as I'd liked the sound of Marc Bolan, Roger Chapman of Family, Captain Beefheart and so on.' A neat link with his past. On another occasion, Peel memorably described the early Cocteau Twins' material as 'sounding as though it might have been produced by a sort of post-punk Phil Spector, wall-of-sound-ish'.

Elsewhere, sessions from the Beat, whose March recordings would be their third and last for the show, Danse Society and Dead Or Alive all proved rather less challenging than many listeners had come to expect.

The following year started with what was by now a rare reggae session, this time from veterans Culture, who recorded their contribution in January. The following month saw Julian Cope record a solo session in the wake of the demise of the Teardrop Explodes, and in March 1983, New Order released another long-term Peel favourite, 'Blue Monday'. Quite possibly the bleakest disco recording ever made, the single simultaneously maintained a dour Northern edge while hinting at a bright techno-future. It was a hugely influential recording – and went on to become the best-selling 12-inch of all time.

All this was merely a prelude to the appearance of a band that would change the face of the decade, though. The emergence of the Smiths, fronted by the inimitable Steven Patrick Morrissey, was assisted in no small part by their early sessions for *The John Peel Show*, but it had been John Walters who had initially decided to follow up the reports he'd heard of the then-unknown Mancunians. Their publicist at the time, Scott Piering, had encouraged Walters to see the band, and on 6 May he did so at the University of London Students' Union. So convinced was he by the experience that the band were offered a session there and then, and the recording was undertaken on 18 May. The performance of 'What Difference Does It Make?' committed to tape that day was markedly different from the version that would emerge as the band's third single – many fans think it superior. There were also versions of 'Miserable Lie', 'Reel Around The Fountain' and 'Handsome Devil', the session enjoying its debut transmission on 31 May. Wildly enthusiastic about the group from the start, Peel repeated the session twice over the summer, while the band went on to record twice for David Jensen's evening show before a second Peel recording in September.

Guitarist Johnny Marr openly acknowledges how crucial these early sessions, and specifically Peel's reaction to the band, were to the Smiths' success: 'They were really important; we wanted to make music for people of our age, 'cause punk had been a few years before and there were young kids looking for something new. We did this session, and it was repeated, like, three or four times, there was a phenomenal reaction to it – Peel was biggin' us up massively. The sessions became . . . our bulletins to our audience, really.'

Once more, the quality of the band's lead voice had much to do with Peel's fervour. Looking back in 1987, Peel commented, 'I liked the fact that I was hearing words being used in popular songs that I wasn't used to hearing. Just the use of language, really, pleased me as much as anything else, and Morrissey's voice wasn't one that you could trace back to anyone else; he wasn't trying to be Marc Bolan or [the Doors'] Jim Morrison again. They arrived as if from nowhere with a very strong identity, and that's always attractive.'

There were other factors in the Smiths' meteoric rise, not least the quality of the songwriting and the attention brought by tabloid outrage at the perceived lyrical content of 'Reel Around The Fountain' (suggestions of paedophiliac overtones to the song, which were later refuted), but there's no doubt that Peel's patronage helped enormously in building their reputation. That second Peel session, recorded in September, included 'This Charming Man', instantly chosen by Rough Trade supremo Geoff Travis to be the band's next single. Between then and November, when the commercially recorded version was released, Peel had repeated the session three times, and this priceless promotion helped to ensure the song's success. 'This Charming Man' effectively presented the Smiths' entire philosophy in one song – nostalgia, beauty and maudlin wit. The world most definitely listened and the rest, as they say, is history.

Another notable debutant in 1983 was the left-wing Bard of Barking, Billy Bragg. The session he recorded on 27 July, transmitted just a week later, caught him in fine form, and included a version of 'A13, Trunk Road To The Sea', the traditional encore to live shows for many a year afterwards. While there were some at Radio One who avoided Bragg's socially and politically aware agit-folk like the plague, presumably fearful for their future prospects, John Peel actively promoted him through a series of sessions that eventually stretched into the early 1990s.

While Bragg's music also found an outlet through the

station's evening shows, it was Peel who provided the biggest platform for the singer's work, no doubt due to his being sympathetic to many of Bragg's political ideas. While he would never have allowed himself to abuse his position of power as a broadcaster by using it as a soapbox for his own political beliefs, Peel consistently demonstrated his socialist principles and concern for the underdog via his support for artists such as Bragg. As the singer himself reflected in 1999, 'The people who worried in the 1980s about playing Billy Bragg records on Radio One – when [Tory politician] Norman Tebbit would ring up and complain – they ain't there anymore. They ain't even in *radio* anymore. But Peel, who didn't worry about his career and just played it 'cause he believed in it – *he's* still there.'

Peel and Walters's office at Egton House was famously something of a shambles, packed with vinyl and tapes and decorated with yellowing Christmas cards dating back years. No amount of complaints from Peel's secretary Sue (known to the duo, for some arcane reason, as Brian) would change matters – nor would the arrival in 1985 of rookie DJ Andy Kershaw, who agreed the office was 'an absolute tip': 'I remember sitting in the office on one occasion, about ten o'clock in the morning, having a cup of coffee when a head comes round the door. A rather bossy woman with a clipboard . . . slaps this piece of paper down on the desk and said, "When Mr Walters gets in, give him this." It was a stiff memorandum to say the office was contravening the Health and Safety at Work Act!' Kershaw was to become one of Peel's most trusted confidants among his fellow broadcasters, and remains on the BBC airwaves today as Radio Three's world music expert.

Towards the end of 1983, a new Channel Four television show had revolutionized music TV in the UK. Vibrant, brash and unpredictable, *The Tube* was the nearest thing to a visual equivalent of John Peel's programme, and remained so until Jools Holland memorably uttered the f-word during a live broadcast in 1987, and the show was unceremoniously axed. Channel Four's advertisers were clearly not amused.

The year following *The Tube*'s arrival saw Peel sessions by Microdisney, the Chameleons, Yeah Yeah Noh and the Mighty Wah! confirm the renaissance of intelligent, guitar-driven music after a fallow year or two. But a new breed of semi-acoustic bands was waiting in the wings to give 1984 a curiously provincial feel. The Boothill Foot Tappers, the Pogues (a bunch of London-based Irish musicians then known as Pogue Mahone) and the Men They Couldn't Hang all brought a fresh, folk-influenced approach that reaffirmed Peel's continuing interest in promoting the more esoteric side of popular music.

Though the Pogues would break through to the radio mainstream – having commuted their original name, which is Gaelic for 'Kiss my arse' – Peel's opinion of Radio One's output and those who span it remained generally low. While his arch nemesis Tony Blackburn had bid the station farewell in 1984, morning DJ Simon Bates, famed for his mawkish 'Our Tune' spot, replaced him in Peel's affections. Peel would often tell the possibly apocryphal story that David Jensen, Paul Burnett and himself, all allegedly the worse for drink, had once waited in the underground BBC car park for the chance to beat Bates up – 'Fortunately he didn't turn up . . . he's probably stronger than us!'

Two bands who would loom large in the John Peel story over the next three years also emerged in 1984, both releasing their first recordings on the new Creation label. First was the Loft, a short-lived and somewhat unstable group that finally disintegrated very publicly, mid-song, during a show at the Hammersmith Palais. Singer and main songwriter Pete Astor and drummer Dave Morgan later worked together in the Weather Prophets, bassist Bill Prince subsequently formed the Wishing Stones, while guitarist Andy Strickland would put together the Caretaker Race. All four new acts were firm *Peel Show* favourites, bringing their melodic brand of indie to countless programmes in the latter part of the decade.

The second Creation band to make an indelible mark in the mid-1980s was the Jesus and Mary Chain, whose debut session in October 1984 gave most listeners their first opportunity to sample the group's unique approach of submerging 1960s-style pop melodies beneath an avalanche of bass and feedback. Drawing inspiration from American noise merchants Hüsker Dü and Sonic Youth, they were the embodiment of rock chic, encased in leather, hidden behind the obligatory rock-star shades and dripping cool, and the mini-riot that attracted *New Musical Express* headlines after one of their early shows did much to enhance this image.

In retrospect, the Mary Chain threatened far more than they ultimately delivered, the constant infighting between founding brothers Jamie and William Reid diluting their creative energy and ultimately proving to be their downfall. Their debut album, *Psychocandy*, however, remains a classic statement of intent, and tracks from the album were a staple of Peel shows during 1985.

One genre heard less and less as the decade passed was reggae, one of Peel's passions since its early origins in the 1960s in ska and bluebeat. Reggae had been in sharp decline since the late 1970s, and, by the mid-1980s there were very few releases he found worthy of airtime. 'Over the last few years,' he observed in typically forthright fashion, 'reggae's been going through a very lean patch. The records have often been formulaic and repetitive, and most important, the actual songs have been utter crap. I'm aware that there's a fine reggae tradition of making it up as you go along, but some of the records are so bad that I really do think that a little forward planning somewhere along the line would have been a good idea!' Bucking the trend in 1985 were the Naturalites, who recorded their second Peel session in May, Maxi Priest, whose debut session went out in March, and recordings by old favourites Misty In Roots and Gregory Isaacs.

The year 1985 brought a succession of fascinating recordings by a wide variety of artists. On 8 January, the Beloved recorded their first Peel session, while in February, a raucous cocktail of jagged guitars, machine-gun percussion and terse vocals announced the arrival of Big Flame, a band whose influence could clearly be heard over the next few years in the work of Twang, A Witness and the Great Leap Forward – all firm favourites of Peel's as the 1980s wore on.

On 5 May, Australian band the Triffids recorded their second set for the show, three country/blues-tinged rock songs that captured the essence of the group before they signed to a major label and somehow lost their edge. It was a pattern Peel had observed over and over again during his time as a DJ. In a 1989 interview, citing the example of Simple Minds, whose early career he'd followed with interest, he remarked, 'There is something in the process of becoming famous that removes from the music what I used to like, and I don't know exactly what it is I like, but it's not there all of a sudden.' Not surprisingly, given their rise from the ashes of his favourites the Undertones, John found exactly what he liked in the triple-guitar-driven political pop of That Petrol Emotion, whose debut session he broadcast in June.

Before helping to put That Petrol Emotion together, ex-Undertones guitarist Damian O'Neill had been involved in one of the more curious sessions to grace the Peel show in 1985. On 24 February, O'Neill, along with Al Thompson (guitar) and David Davies (bass), had been part of Dawn Chorus and the Blue Tits, featuring future Radio One DJ Liz Kershaw as the vocalist. Liz's brother Andy also got in on the act, whistling on one of the session's four tracks, among which was a version of 'Teenage Kicks'! (In a return to his Shrewsbury schooldays, John himself would pluck tea-chest bass for an equally short-lived assemblage of skiffling Radio One presenters, including Andy Kershaw and John Walters, which appeared on the *Old Grey Whistle Test* that November.)

On a more serious note, the same year saw the Smiths unleash the classic album *Meat Is Murder*, Prefab Sprout release *Steve McQueen* and the Wedding Present offer their debut single 'Go Out And Get 'Em Boy' on their own Reception Records in May, all three well worth the attention they received through the programme. (The Wedding Present in particular would become firm Peel favourites, and their singer/guitarist David Gedge a personal friend; his later group Cinerama would be among the select acts invited to play sessions at Peel Acres.)

For John, though, 1985 was blighted by the tragic events that unfolded before his horrified gaze in the Heysel Stadium in Belgium, where his beloved Liverpool were due to take on Juventus in the European Cup Final. Thirty-nine Juventus fans died after a wall collapsed close to where John and Sheila were waiting to watch the game, and, unsurprisingly, this had a profound effect on him. For years afterwards he would have a fear of crowds, so much so that he stopped going to Liverpool games altogether, something that would have been unthinkable a short time earlier.

Although he would say little in public about the disaster in the years that followed, there is no doubt that in private John felt deeply saddened by the needless waste of life. Above all else, John Peel was a caring individual – he cared passionately about music, he cared deeply about his family and, no matter how famous he became, he never stopped caring about ordinary people.

Late in October, Bogshed taped the first of the five sessions they would eventually complete for the programme. The band became one of innumerable footnotes in musical history, but they proved the world was listening as intently to Peel as ever. When he described Bogshed as 'shambling', he couldn't have dreamed that the music press would pick up on his comments with such enthusiasm that the term would come to define a whole genre. It prompted the following explanation during the *Peeling Back The Years* series: 'On several occasions since I've apologized to the members of Bogshed for lumbering them with this "shambling" business. They were the band I was speaking of when I first used the expression on the radio. What I was trying to imply was that they were a band whose preoccupations were not necessarily with either developing extraordinary musical skills, or with international celebrity. It was an attempt to describe an attitude, an approach they had which made them sound attractively disorganized.'

Less than two weeks after Bogshed's initial airing, another attractively disorganized band made their debut on the show. Half Man Half Biscuit were an irreverent bunch of off-the-wall Liverpudlians whose humorous songs drew their inspiration from popular culture – numbers such as 'The Trumpton Riots' and 'I Hate Nerys Hughes' featured frequently on the show over the next few years.

The 'shambling' bands provided many of the most interesting sessions heard over the coming months, with debuts by A Witness, Stump, Twang and the MacKenzies all to be heard during January and February 1986. While all these bands tended towards a jagged, angular style, characterized by snappy basslines, staccato percussion and jangly guitars, Stump were out on their own, challenging notions of what music could sound like in a way reminiscent of Captain Beefheart a dozen or so years earlier. Never likely to make any commercial impact, Stump nevertheless went on to record three further Peel sessions.

Other session debutants of 1986 were Pop Will Eat Itself and the gloriously named all-female quartet We've Got A Fuzzbox And We're Gonna Use It, while long-term favourites the Fall were enjoying a particularly creative period, tracks from the previous year's *This Nation's Saving Grace* and their new album *Bend Sinister* regularly making the playlist. After two excellent sessions in 1985, they recorded yet another, their thirteenth, in July 1986. Even by then, though, Peel and Mark E. Smith had yet to develop more than a distant relationship.

This year also marked a breakthrough for the Wedding Present, who aroused more interest among listeners with their second single 'Once More' than with their first a year earlier. With the Housemartins, the Bodines, the Weather Prophets, the Primitives and the Shop Assistants, 1986 proved to be a vintage year, but it wasn't all down to guitar-based rock. Once again, new musical forms were making their presence felt, with Run-DMC, Mantronix, Troublefunk, and other rising stars in the hip-hop firmament pushing to be heard.

With its origins among deprived black kids in America, hip-hop was indie's most unlikely bedfellow, but Peel, with his customary disregard for continuity or context, played this rapidly emerging music alongside the more established fare, to unexpected effect. Letters of complaint started coming in once more, in much the same way as they had almost twenty years earlier when he had dared to play ska singles, and ten years previously when punk had swept the old order away. Naturally, this hostility simply served to confirm that here was a phenomenon worth further investigation and, over the next two or three years the genre became a firmly established part of the programme.

The calculated industry gamble that teamed up Run–DMC and classic rockers Aerosmith for 'Walk This Way' that autumn did much to bring hip-hop into the mainstream, but Peel continued to play cutting-edge material in his show through acts such as LL Cool J, Eric B and Rakim, EPMD and Stetsasonic. Biggest of all would be Public Enemy, a spitting, snarling hip-hop conglomerate whose 1987 debut album *Yo! Bum Rush The Show* was both a musical and political tour de force, a powerful statement of their intent to raise black awareness. As the 1980s drew to a close, Public Enemy's following albums, *It Takes A Nation Of Millions To Hold Us Back* and *Fear Of A Black Planet* continued to provide some of the hardest hip-hop to feature on the Peel playlist.

John later remarked how satisfying it was when he received letters from listeners along the lines of 'I was one of those who wrote to you a year or so back to say don't play any more hip-hop, but I've just realized that the last six records I've bought were all hip-hop, so I guess you were right.' In many ways, he'll probably be remembered most for dragging some of his audience kicking and screaming into the jaws of punk, but Peel deserves equal credit for successfully introducing his largely white, indie-oriented listenership to the wonders of hip-hop, reggae and techno, parts of the musical spectrum most of them had initially considered unworthy of attention.

By the end of 1986, John had all but stopped co-hosting *Top of the Pops*, and made just one appearance the following year, in February. There was a watershed incident, as he later recalled: 'When I took the children stock-car racing in Ipswich this chap came up and said, "Aren't you the bloke from the telly?"

It says a lot about Britain, really, that newsreaders, weathermen and DJs are seen as cultural icons. I thought, "I'm not the bloke off the telly, I'm their dad!" so I stopped.' Ironically, if anyone from the UK media community could be regarded as a cultural icon it was Peel. From now on, he would restrict his small-screen activities to voice-overs for commercials before extending his TV activities in the mid-1990s to include narrating programmes such as *A Life of Grime*.

As the world outside boogied beneath the newly discovered hole in the ozone layer to a soap-opera soundtrack penned by Stock, Aitken and Waterman, 1987 saw yet more fascinating developments in alternative music. Not surprisingly, Peel's show continued to bring its listeners the pick of the crop.

Sampling was fast becoming a bone of contention within the industry, with accusations of aural theft and threats of legal action flying back and forth. Peel found the concept both refreshing and challenging, featuring an increasing amount of both rap and hip-hop in his shows, although he was still having to work hard to counter criticism of the genres from his die-hard fans.

'How people can say it all sounds the same, or that it's boring, I simply don't know,' he argued. 'I mean, the structure of a conventional rock song tends to mean that the song sounds much the same all the way through – it's guitar, bass, drums and somebody singing – but with hip-hop there are so many elements brought into play, and brought in from so many random points – sampled speech, sampled rhythms, sampled guitar, that there's huge amounts going on. In fact,' he went on, 'there's almost too much happening on some of the records, and you have to listen to them quite carefully and quite a lot to be able to identify everything that's going on.'

It was inevitable that Peel, now a happily domesticated father to four young children when not on duty at the BBC, would occasionally find his tastes merging with those of his children. So it was that he and his eldest son, William, then around twelve, found themselves en route to a 'hip-hop convention' at Wembley Arena. There they met a star DJ known as DJ Cheese, whose much-prized autograph was, for many years, prominently on view at Peel Acres. Whom could his kids rely upon to shock such a hip dad? 'Andrew Lloyd Webber' came the answer, through gritted teeth. As far as is known, however, showertime renditions of *Evita* and *Jesus Christ Superstar* in the Suffolk area were few and far between ...

At the time, John was also becoming increasingly interested in what has become known as 'world music', a term he found impossible to embrace for reasons he would set out whenever the subject was raised: 'I can never understand why people are so desperate to stamp some kind of group identity on to all these things, because as far as I'm concerned someone like, say, the Butthole Surfers, is as much "world music" as whatever people pigeonhole as "world music" – the Bhundu Boys, or whoever. It's all simply good, or bad, or exciting, or not exciting.'

As always, he had a point – on 23 February 1988, Peel dedicated his entire programme to music from around the globe, featuring Kafka (from Brazil), Touche A L'Arabe (Germany), Madame (Poland), Dazibao (Franco-Algerian) and Kidderiko (Japan) alongside items from the countries more generally associated with the term – Africa and Asia. It was a bold move, and one that demonstrated John's strongly held belief that music is a global language.

The Peel programme was to play an important part in championing another genre during 1987, as British hardcore began to get up a head of steam. During the closing weeks of the previous year, a number of tracks from the debut album by the Stupids had been aired on the programme and, on 9 December 1986 the band recorded the first of their three Peel sessions. Soon after it was transmitted on 12 January 1987, Peel and Walters saw the band, and two others which included one or more members of the Stupids, perform in Fulham. Peel reviewed the gig in the following Sunday's *Observer*, noting that their performance was characterized by commendable brevity and lack of attention to detail: 'It was like punk all over again.' The two other bands were Bad Dress Sense and Frankfurter, both of whom were invited to record for the show.

After a short respite, the hardcore hurricane picked up again in July, when the Electro Hippies recorded their only session. Startling was too meagre a word for it – nine tracks, none more than 1 minute 40 seconds in length, and the last, 'Mega Armageddon Death' clocking in at just one second. On the session sheet, producer Dale Griffin noted pithily, 'Stops and starts rather abruptly.' Something of an understatement, perhaps? John Walters was now spending an increasing amount of time looking for new hardcore bands at the few London venues which supported the genre, and there was a steady stream of new music to enjoy. Heresy recorded the first of their three sessions in July, but in September the BBC studios played host to Napalm Death, whose debut comprised twelve songs totalling under six minutes, making it the shortest-ever Peel session. By contrast, the first by Gore, recorded in November '87, included a seventeen-minute medley of four songs, along with a second number lasting almost eight minutes. There were already wide differences between the movement's leading lights.

Away from the hardcore scene, Big Black – an uncompromising American trio led by the prickly Steve Albini – recorded an explosive session for the programme in late April, and as summer arrived so did Cud, indie-popsters from Leeds signed to the Wedding Present's Reception label, whose June debut included a spirited, if unlikely, romp through Hot Chocolate's 'You Sexy Thing'. The Sugarcubes, featuring the diminutive Björk as lead vocalist, burst on to the scene with their spine-tingling debut single 'Birthday', and the Shamen offered 'Christopher Mayhew Says', an acid-rock blockbuster overlaid with samples of MP Christopher Mayhew's commentary on an acid trip he took for research purposes in the 1950s. Both bands would go on to greater things in the early 1990s, although the Shamen would do so as a dance act, while Björk was to achieve wider success as a solo artist. The curiously named 'grebo' scene brought the Wonder Stuff, Gaye Bikers On Acid and Crazyhead, while M/A/R/R/S pumped up the volume to make history as the first record produced on an independently distributed label to reach the number-one spot.

The final thread running through 1987 and into 1988 was the presence of a growing number of bands who were not only from Wales, but sang in Welsh. Like hardcore, the first stirrings had been felt during the previous year, starting with a session from Anhrefn, whose eponymous label later issued records by many of the most significant Welsh-speaking bands. Peel enthusiastically supported the groups involved, although he worried that his interest might be misconstrued. When he included Datblygu's 'Wyau' in a 1988 list of records he felt should have been more successful, he was moved to explain: 'This feels like I'm doing my good deed for all the oppressed minorities in pop music. Essentially, though, I don't accept that this kind of record would be of minority interest if they were heard by more people. I get very frustrated with people's inability to see what's going on under their noses. Obviously, being a Welsh-language band, Datblygu are automatically a "minority concern", but to me this is worthy of a wider audience.'

He needn't have worried, as Gorwel Owen of Plant Bach Ofnus told John Robb in a 1988 interview for *Sounds*: 'Peel has been really helpful. After his session, we got a German tour and a record deal, plus there's been a lot of interest in the band. People have accused him of being tokenist in his interest in the Welsh scene, but that's not the case. He actually phoned Datblygu, worried that he may have been seen to be patronizing, but this is simply not true.' The last three years of the decade featured both sessions and records by a number of Welsh-speaking bands, including Anhrefn (punk), Plant Bach Ofnus (a post–Cabaret Voltaire synthesizer duo), Traddodiad Ofnus (punk, metallic clatter and quirky pop), Datblygu (at times reminiscent of the Fall), Llwybr Llaethog (skewed hip-hop) and Fflaps. One band, Heb Gared from Newport, actually learned Welsh in order to make a Welsh-language record.

In 1988, Bolt Thrower, Doom and Carcass kept hardcore in the Peel spotlight, while Public Enemy ensured hip-hop didn't fade from view either. House music began to make its presence felt, and once more Peel was in the vanguard, giving airtime to A Guy Called Gerald and the Funky Ginger during the course of the year. A steady stream of guitar bands kept coming as well, and the show gave vital exposure to the Pixies, who recorded no fewer than three Peel sessions in 1988, and whose quiet-loud-quiet-loud formula provided the blueprint for much of what followed in the early 1990s – most famously, Nirvana.

Ron Johnson and 4AD were the indie labels of the year, the former boasting A Witness, the Great Leap Forward and Jackdaw With Crowbar, the latter the Pixies, Dead Can Dance and Xymox. The September label brought militant communists McCarthy, who produced two classic EPs in 1988, *This Nelson Rockerfeller* and *Should The Bible Be Banned?* Brimful of intelligent political arguments wedded to bitter-sweet melodies, McCarthy were subversive in the same way as Peel himself.

Chinhoyi Superstars' 'Woiteyiko?' was another record that appeared on Peel's list of 'ones that got away'. Defending his choice, he said: 'You may think I'm being deliberately obscure here, but I genuinely think this is highly likeable pop music. It may be from Zimbabwe, but there's nothing remotely distant or alienating about it. I love the endless, ringing guitars, and I can never understand it when people say (as they do of reggae) that it "all sounds the same". I mean, have they listened to it? They are cutting themselves off from a whole sphere of human activity and in effect it's a manifestation of the same prejudice that says "All black men are going to rob you" or certain women saying "All men are rapists." It's awful, and I know that I'm guilty of it myself.' Asked in what way, Peel instantly replied with tongue firmly in cheek, 'I won't allow Arsenal supporters in the house.'

In October, *The John Peel Show* moved to an earlier time, 8.30 p.m. instead of 10 p.m. It was the first change in the scheduling of the show for more than ten years, and had the effect of increasing his audience figures overnight. It was a move that seemed almost to come as a surprise to the host: 'It's always difficult when these things happen because you're obviously not privy to their [the higher authorities'] thought processes. They tell you a certain amount, but not everything. So you end up like a bloke having a bit of a swim, knowing that there's a shark out there somewhere, but not sure where the bugger is.'

He successfully avoided the shark throughout his thirty-seven years at Radio One. And one of the reasons, quite clearly, was John Walters, with whom he enjoyed a working relationship of more than two decades. Peel reflected on his producer some years later with undisguised affection: 'I always characterized the relationship between Walters and myself – and he would probably agree, although he disagrees with most of the things I say – as like a man and his dog, each believing the other to be the dog! It worked very well; he was very skilful in debate, and within the awful meetings you had with the BBC, with management, and so on, he could out-argue them easily. I just got on with sorting out the records and the music, and he took care of business.'

As the decade, a relatively placid one in contrast to its predecessor, entered its final year, Peel was heading towards his fiftieth birthday but showing no sign whatsoever of mellowing or slowing down. Much to his annoyance, Manchester was, yet again, the centre of the musical universe, with acts such as the Happy Mondays, Inspiral Carpets and the Stone Roses unavoidable for most of the year. Another wave of American bands was coming through, with the Sub Pop label releasing records by Tad, Mudhoney, the Afghan Whigs, Les Thugs and the Screaming Trees. In the early 1990s, the label would offer Fugazi, Babes In Toyland and Dinosaur Jr, but their most important discovery was Nirvana – of whom more later.

Four years on from Heysel, disaster again struck at a Liverpool game when ninety-six Liverpool fans died at an FA Cup semi-final at Hillsborough in Sheffield, due to overcrowding on the terraces. Peel opened his first post-Hillsborough show with Aretha Franklin's titanic version of 'You'll Never Walk Alone' before bursting into tears on air. 'Yes, but who wouldn't?' he said later. 'I had to play something. My wife and I were in the Heysel Stadium, very close to where all the people died, [and] we just stood there watching them all being crushed to death. When Hillsborough happened, I'd had an invitation to the match, but I'd not actually been to a match since Heysel. Since then I find crowds of any sort really scary.'

No one who heard the opening moments of that programme would ever forget it. Peel's humanity shone through, as fellow DJ Nicky Campbell later reflected: 'The Monday evening show after the Hillsborough tragedy was a piece of broadcasting I'll never forget. He said nothing at the start of his show. He just played a record. A long, slow record. It was Aretha Franklin's heartbreaking gospel version of 'You'll Never Walk Alone'. I looked through the glass from the adjacent studio and John was just weeping. Silently. So were all of us – all his listeners. Nothing more needed to be said.' Peel himself offered a final postscript some years later: 'Until then, I had no idea it was possible to feel so much grief over the deaths of people I never knew.'

Happier times were to follow later in the year, when friends organized a fiftieth birthday party at London's Subteranea club and arranged for the Fall, the Wedding Present and others to play. An article in *New Musical Express* described the evening, observing Peel's embarrassment at being the centre of so much adulation, and the fact that he (characteristically) shed a tear or two at being presented with an award for being a 'decent bloke'. Guy Chadwick, of the House of Love, acknowledged his group's debt to the man: 'Last year we played to about eighty people at a gig in Leeds which Peel reviewed two days later in the *Observer*, saying we were great. Then he plugged our album for what seemed like weeks and weeks, and had us into the studio for three sessions. His support was just so influential in the success we had last year.'

Ian McCulloch agreed, adding: 'He's the total business. The Bunnymen did lots of sessions for his show; those trips up and down to London in the van were some of the best times we ever had, and I reckon those sessions were some of the best things we ever did.'

For his part, Peel simply said, 'I like to think that I'll be doing radio programmes in ten years' time and thinking a lot of the stuff I'm playing now is crap.' Here was the crucial factor in his longevity – not only was he capable of reassessing the past, he was never going to become one of those people who get to a certain age and decide that they know what they like, and like what they know.

As the 1980s came to a close, Peel remained a flickering beacon of light from outside the safe, cosy world of corporate pop broadcasting. Indeed, he regarded keeping things cosy as anathema, as he'd already explained in *Peeling Back The Years*: 'I don't think you should always necessarily enjoy popular music – this is one of the conflicts I've had with many people over the years. Look at it this way: not every play has a happy ending, not every film you see has a happy ending, and not every painting you look at is going to be of kittens sitting in a basket. I always think the best records and the best gigs are like when I saw the Butthole Surfers for the first time, and I came away thinking "Actually, I don't know if that was any good or not!" You find all your prejudices and preconceptions are laid waste in the space of an hour, and that's vital to one's development.'

At fifty, and describing himself as 'dangerously free of ambition', his deadpan delivery, anti-celebrity stance and self-deprecating humour were all still intact, all essential ingredients of his ability to influence generations of more adventurous listeners by the simple expedient of playing them new music and treating them like intelligent adults.

9

Honours and Home Truths

AFTER A DECADE of Margaret Thatcher, the BBC stood in the 1990s as an Aunt Sally for anyone to take a pot-shot at. And Radio One, the channel on the network most obviously ripe for privatization, was taking more than its fair share of flak from the free marketeers. Why, the critics mused as the Beeb's 'charter renewal' was debated in the early 1990s, should the general public fund a 'yoof' radio station when the likes of Capital (in London) and Virgin did the job without a shred of taxpayers' (or indeed licence-payers') money?

In a curious way, this debate made Peel's position at Radio One as safe as houses. Which commercial station, the BBC's supporters argued, would give a man in his fifties carte blanche to play whatever way-out sounds he wanted without let or hindrance? Worth the licence fee in itself, surely!

Nevertheless, in 1993 radical changes were made to the station following the resignation of Johnny Beerling – who had been Controller of Radio One for eight years and associated with the BBC for thirty-five – and the arrival of youthful Controller-Designate Matthew Bannister. Beerling departed with some bitterness, claiming working at the current BBC was like 'life under Communism'. He complained of 'total control from the centre and very little flexibility or room for manoeuvre'.

Little surprise, then, that Bannister proposed wholesale changes, the like of which had not been seen for nearly two decades. They rivalled the swingeing cuts of 1975 that had seen so many of the 'old guard' depart, and were intended to reflect a lowering of the target audience age range. Many of the established presenters were sacked or resigned and a new breed recruited. The short-term result was, predictably, a loss of listeners. Ratings plunged by 30 per cent in a matter of a few months, and the tabloids, especially the *Sun*, had a field day, depicting Bannister sliding down . . . a staircase banister!

The biggest headlines came when wisecracking 'Hairy Cornflake' Dave Lee Travis resigned on-air in August, ending twenty-six years as a Radio One stalwart. 'Changes are being made which go against my principles,' he declared, 'and I just cannot agree with them. [I] could not continue to work for the station under current circumstances . . . the only option is very regrettably for me to leave – so that is what I am doing.'

The *Guardian* reported with wry humour that 'As DLT packs his record box and prepares to leave Radio One he will leave behind a slight feeling of vulnerability among some of his twenty fellow disc jockeys.' And that feeling proved to be well founded. Other big names to bite the dust in that earth-shaking year of 1993 included fifteen-year veteran Tommy Vance (aged fifty), who joined up-and-coming Virgin Radio, Alan 'Fluff' Freeman (sixty-six), who was shunted over to Radio Two, Johnnie Walker (forty-eight), who eventually ended up at the same destination, and Gary Davies (thirty-four).

For Bob Harris, at the age of forty-six, the axe was particularly hard as he'd also been a victim of the 1975 cull. But it was, he was assured, nothing personal. 'We're repositioning the network,' Bannister told the man who'd been filling the overnight slot, 'moving Radio One forward . . . and expanding the music base.' The latter comment came as a particular snub to 'Whispering Bob', who believed his shows to be 'the most eclectic on the network'.

The year 1993 also saw the Radio One session enshrined in history thanks to *In Session Tonight*, a book by radio journalist Ken Garner, which Peel, in his introduction, rightly praised as 'a work of almost lunatic scholarship'. Garner and Peel had met in 1986 when the former, then a research student at Glasgow University, secured an audience over a curry. The result had been intended for his radio column in the student newspaper, but kicked off a career as a freelance writer (for the *Listener*, among others) and, seven years later, resulted in a book that boasted of the inclusion of 'every Peel session broadcast'.

In Session Tonight may have appeared at a seismic time in Radio One's history, but thankfully it was not to prove any kind of obituary notice, either for Peel or the session format. Clive Selwood had formed a new label, Strange Fruit, in the late 1980s with the intention of releasing the choicest sessions on disc, but time and again would be thwarted by record companies (a Fall box-set remains mired in red tape, despite the band's approval) and even, sometimes, artists, who either wanted too much money or flatly refused to let their work reach the public by legal means. Needless to say, unofficial cassette tapes of Peel sessions had been circulating for decades among the rabid fans who would have comprised the market for such music.

Peel's first major musical discovery of the decade came in

October 1991 when he was employed as guest reviewer by *Melody Maker*. Happening across the debut single by West Country girl Polly Jean Harvey, he promptly made it his 'Single of the Week'. (He didn't realize it then, but the recording in question, 'Dress', came from the demo tape Harvey had submitted to her label, Too Pure – perhaps John just had a nose for demo tapes.)

A Peel session invitation quickly followed – so speedily, in fact, that it was broadcast that November, and a further five would chart P. J. Harvey's progress for the rest of the decade as she climbed aboard a major label and rose to Top Three album status. Her take on the singer-songwriter genre was refreshingly in-your-face, a fact that enthralled Peel; on the other hand, she wasn't averse to using high heels among her stage props, something that achieved an equally enthusiastic response from her male fans.

Nirvana, the pioneering grunge trio from Seattle, were another Peel-championed force to be reckoned with at this time. As ever, he had been the first in the UK to play their music, airing their first Sub Pop single 'Love Buzz'/'Big Cheese' soon after its late-1988 release. A session the following year, before the band had replaced drummer Chad Channing with Dave Grohl, would be followed by two more in 1990 and 1991, the latter being so informal that the band felt free enough to debut a song new enough to be logged as 'No Title As Yet'! By the time of leader Kurt Cobain's sad demise in 1994, they had passed into superstardom and thus far from Peel's boundaries, their final Radio One session being for Mark Goodier.

As Radio One contemplated its future under Matthew Bannister, the stage was set for the return of Trevor Dann, who'd produced *The John Peel Show* for a few weeks in 1983 before graduating to television and the *Old Grey Whistle Test*;

he encountered Peel again on his return to radio a dozen years later as the grandly titled Head of Production. By that time John had forgiven him for an earlier misdemeanour, which occurred when Dann placed a cup of coffee too close to Peel's cueing arm so that a stray elbow sent it cascading into the mixing desk, necessitating a swift change of studio . . .

Dann's job description was said by some to be Bannister's 'enforcer', suggesting a 'party line' in matters of musical taste. In March 1996, he nailed his colours to the mast by reportedly saying, 'If I go down in history as the man who stopped Radio One playing crap records then I shall be a proud man.' Twelve-bar veterans Status Quo received an airplay ban they threatened to test by legal means, while the 'new' Beatles single 'Real Love' (fabricated by Electric Light Orchestra mastermind Jeff Lynne from a John Lennon demo tape and released in March 1996 to promote the second volume of the Fab Four's *Anthology*), was deemed unlikely to be played on Radio One – even though a tabloid 'taste test' suggested over 90 per cent of its readers disagreed with that decision. (It reached number four anyway, with or without the avuncular Dann's approval.)

Trevor Dann admitted to several arguments with Peel, who was now having to fight his own battles since John Walters had moved away from radio production into new television and radio ventures in the early 1990s – yet it had been Dann who'd given John the freedom to sequence the show as he wanted in 1983, a task that until then had remained with the producer as a throwback to a bygone age.

The ferment behind the scenes at Radio One provided material aplenty for Simon Garfield's book, *The Nation's Favourite: The True Adventures of Radio One*, published in 1998 – and this in turn was adapted as a one-man play staged at that year's Edinburgh Festival. Bannister, by then an ex-Controller and now a Radio Five presenter, was very taken with the result and attempted to interest comedian Steve Coogan in making a TV version, though this never actually materialized.

Peel's position among the DJ hierarchy had rarely been threatened, but the mass changes of 1993 brought a young pretender into the Radio One fold in the shape of Steve Lamacq. The Bournemouth-born presenter had trained as a journalist on a local paper and shared a love of football with Peel; indeed, he became sports editor of the *Harlow Gazette* at the age of only twenty-one.

Like Peel, Lamacq had a record label in his life – albeit one more commercially successful than Dandelion – in the shape of Deceptive Records, formed in 1992 with friends Tony Smith and Alan James. The highest-profile band to emerge on the label was Elastica, but ironically their success caused Lamacq to leave the company after the release of their first album (*Elastica*, March 1995), to avoid accusations of nepotism. It reached number one anyway.

In fact, Peel had been keener on Blur, led by singer-guitarist Damon Albarn. Indicating how incestuous the scene was, Elastica singer Justine Frischmann, who'd briefly been in another fast-rising band, Suede, was Albarn's long-term girlfriend. Ironically, she would be sued by perennial Peel favourites Wire, who argued that one of her songs borrowed rather too freely from one of their earlier works.

Lamacq's path to Broadcasting House took in *New Musical Express*, a route that would soon bring in another young hopeful in the shape of ebullient Wiganite Stuart Maconie. Lamacq joined Radio One in September 1993, initially as co-presenter of *The Evening Session* with Jo Whiley – but, just as with Peel in 1976, was destined for greater things and had piloted the show on his own from February 1997. Peel was clearly taken by the youngster, a full quarter of a century his junior, bestowing on him the nickname 'Lammo', but was less than amused when he discovered in 1995 that his pal was to supersede him as host of the Reading Festival.

'I was very hurt by that,' conceded Peel, who actually learned the news while reading a paper at that summer's Glastonbury Festival. 'If they'd said to me "You're out of sympathy with most of the bands and we'd sooner get in someone else to do it," then that would have been fine. As it was, I was given the unofficial word that I was doing it again until one of the children bought me the paper with the line-up for Reading in it and it said, "Compère and DJ on the main stage: Steve Lamacq."'

Indeed, Lamacq went on to front most of Radio One's live-music festival coverage, although Peel kept tight personal hold of Glastonbury by developing a 'beauty and the beast' television partnership with Steve's former co-host Jo Whiley. This could lead to some interesting conversations since, as Whiley recalled, Peel would be fuelled on red wine while she topped up with Jack Daniel's: 'We'd have quite a lot of heated debates about different bands. I'd be getting really excited about who's on the main stage, the headline act – "REM are on stage; Coldplay are on stage" – and he'd be going "Huh" and just grumbling, 'cause John grumbled; he was good at grumbling. And he'd be like, "Huh, don't know what you see in them," and he'd be shouting about Kanda Bongo Man or somebody completely obscure that I knew nothing about ...'

Another famous exchange between the two, one that should probably not have taken place in front of a live audience, concerned Icelandic singer Björk – like Jack Daniel's, an acquired taste. When Jo Whiley asked John what he'd been up to, he replied that he'd had far too much red wine and been to see Björk. 'So what did you think of her, then?' asked Whiley. 'I just can't stand all that "I'm a little pixie" shit she does!' slurred Peel. 'Er, okay. Moving on . . .'

The Britpop wars of 1995, when Blur and Oasis raced each other to the top of the singles charts and made the lead story on the BBC television news, were something that Peel resolutely avoided. Indeed, while he'd championed Blur since the early 1990s, he'd never given Oasis the time of day, believing that what they did had been done better before. Yet as Steve Lamacq reflected after Peel's death: 'It's strange . . . people say Peel didn't play a huge role in Britpop, but he was in fact the godfather of it, in a way, because he'd been championing all the music that led up to it.'

Pulp, the commercially unviable bunch of characters from Sheffield led by the nerdy, bespectacled Jarvis Cocker, certainly repaid Peel's faith, re-emerging at this point and reaching the top of the charts nearly a decade and a half after their first Peel session in 1981.

Peel also introduced Sunderland-based band Kenickie to the airwaves in the mid-1990s. Their invigorating punk-pop energy duly earned them a cult following within the UK music press even before their debut album was released, and two John Peel sessions later followed. Former lead singer Lauren Laverne is now an award-winning DJ on XFM, a radio station fashioned in Peel's image. And if imitation is the sincerest form of flattery, then XFM should surely have paid the man royalties. The London-based commercial radio station started as a pirate playing the kind of alternative music with which Peel had become synonymous, before going 'legit' in September 1997.

In August 1998, however, XFM's freedom to play whatever it wanted was removed by its acquisition by the Capital Radio group. A group of enraged 'anoraks' picketed outside Capital's Leicester Square office, where Ricky Gervais, now a small-screen superstar thanks to *The Office* but then an XFM presenter, tried to rouse them via a megaphone – all, of course, to no avail. If anyone needed persuading that John Peel could only have existed on the BBC, despite his many battles with the Corporation, they merely had to compare XFM's pre- and post-takeover output. Indeed, just two months after their change of ownership they were hit with a fine by the Radio Authority for not keeping to their PoP (Promise of Performance, a document created when a station is given its licence).

In fairness, XFM has since got its act together somewhat. Their *X-Posure Live* show plays unsigned bands and gave Athlete, the Thrills and Razorlight their first airplay. The Libertines, Franz Ferdinand and many others were booked for early sessions, while live recordings featured on a daily basis and were therefore accessible by those Londoners unable to listen to Peel's late-night slot.

XFM inevitably became a 'feeder' station, supplying BBC Radio with a production line of new presenters, Adam and Joe, Richard Bacon and Zoë Ball among them. And, in July 2003, it yielded a new figure in the Lamacq/Peel mould, in the form of New Zealander Zane Lowe, who reputedly cost Radio One a hefty 'transfer fee' when he signed on the line to present its Tuesday to Thursday 8–10 p.m. shows.

The new acquisition was the brainchild of Radio One's latest controller, Andy Parfitt, who'd replaced Matthew Bannister in 1998 and seen off the likes of DJs Kevin Greening and Simon Mayo, as well as exiling Andy Kershaw to an after-midnight slot. Zane Lowe's arrival was bad news for Steve Lamacq, though, whose *Evening Session* came to an end in December 2000.

Happily, Peel's relationship with former protégé Bob Harris underwent an overhaul in the 1990s. Though Harris wasn't to rejoin his one-time best friend on the Radio One roster, his continuing taste for American music, particularly the country-rock (now known as alt-country) genre, made him a natural for the repositioned Radio Two.

In his autobiography, Harris confirmed that, since his return to the Corporation, he appeared to have 'rehabilitated myself in John's opinion. He's become a fan of *Bob Harris Country* and told me recently [in 2001] that he listens to the programme driving home to Suffolk on Thursday nights. He's been writing about me again, in his column in *Radio Times*.' The pair also enjoyed a musical overlap for the first time in years, championing the likes of alt-country artists Laura Cantrell, Calexico and Radio Sweethearts. 'It feels good to have Peel approval again,' whispered the now happily remarried Harris, adding, 'he's still in a class of his own.'

In 1998, Peel was invited to curate the Meltdown Festival, a week of concerts at London's Royal Festival Hall that had been running for four years; other members of the music aristocracy to have taken charge include David Bowie, Scott Walker and Morrissey. Unfortunately for such a devout sports-lover as John, the week coincided with football's World Cup in France. He countered this clash by ensuring all the major games were visible via a giant video screen in the foyer.

The Tuesday night concert on 30 June was delayed, however, while England crashed out of the competition against Argentina in St Etienne, France. The match went to extra time and penalties, with the knock-on result that Gorky's Zygotic Mynci, the first of two headline acts, didn't take the stage until well after 11 p.m. Cornershop, the co-headliners, arrived at past midnight. Their hit 'Brimful Of Asha' had topped the poll in the previous year's Festive Fifty – though, due to a disappointing response from his listeners,

Peel had commuted the rundown to just thirty-one records. But the happy, Asian-flavoured music made people forget their World Cup disappointment (though the sight of Liverpool's teen prodigy Michael Owen scoring with a run from the halfway line had already done the trick for John).

Throughout the 1990s, Peel's health had become a source of worry both to himself and Sheila – though, as with so many men of middle age, he'd seemed to take great steps to avoid confronting his fears. Tiredness and blurred vision had been two recent complaints, and so he finally went for a medical assessment on 11 September 2001. Watching the planes hit the World Trade Center put his problem – diabetes – into perspective. Peel was told that he would have to ensure he ate only at certain times of the day in the future – not a prospect that filled him with delight: 'It's a bugger. I've always been overweight, I'll concede that, but it's a bigger job just keeping your weight as it is.' As well as having to control his middle-aged spread, he now also had the undignified task of stabbing it with hypodermic insulin needles.

Yet all this was as nothing to the shock he'd felt a few years earlier when in 1996, his beloved Sheila had suffered a brain haemorrhage. As luck would have it, he had been away from home when it happened, at the TT races on the Isle of Man, though afterwards he revealed that he had had a premonition of the event. Andy Kershaw, who had been with him, accompanied Peel to the mainland and provided invaluable support. 'Andy stayed with me all the way to the hospital,' Peel later recalled. 'I'll never forget how sympathetic, yet firm, he was.'

The family rallied round and the Pig made a full recovery, but it had been a frightening experience, one that Peel would recall daily. 'I remember the terrible emptiness I felt,' he'd later recount, 'when the children and I were waiting in the hospital for the brain surgery to finish. I didn't cry – I was somewhere beyond crying . . . As I waited for the ferry, I stood on the cliffs above Douglas and just howled into the night.'

The importance of continued health and well-being was further thrown into sharp focus with the death of John Walters in 2001. His funeral was, in Clive Selwood's words, 'A riot of music and laughter, which was a fair reflection of a remarkable personality.' Peel was writing a weekly column in the *Radio Times* at the time, *Sounds* music paper having long since bitten the dust, and by total coincidence had written a eulogy to his friend and former producer that had appeared in print the very week of his passing; Walters had seemed in the best of health at the time of writing nearly a month previously – a suspected heart attack was believed to be the cause of his sudden demise.

The BBC (which had shed Radio One's medium-wave frequency in 1994, leaving it FM-only) was keen to make a dent in the new world of digital radio, and created 6 Music in March 2002 as an eclectic channel that encompassed presenters as diametrically opposed as Iron Maiden heavy-metal screamer Bruce Dickinson, roly-poly comic Phill Jupitus and former gay rocker (though now happily married and a father) Tom Robinson. Whether the powers that be might have seen this as a possible home for Peel should they have dared shunt him off Radio One is unknown, but the musical freedoms the presenters wielded had to be weighed against the fact that digital radio was then, and remains now, a medium listened to by single-figure percentages of the public.

Instead, John had made a sideways move to Radio Four, where his presentation of *Home Truths* (according to John, 'a name chosen only when it became an administrative impossibility for programme-planning to continue without a name') drew one and a half million listeners each and every Saturday morning – no mean feat for a programme his pal Andy Kershaw thought 'cloying, sentimental and indulgent'.

It clearly struck a chord with others, however, and in some ways was an extension of Peel's *Radio Times* column. This had rejoiced in the title of *John Peel's Family Album* (until, apparently, his children objected to their home life being strewn across the pages of a nationally circulated listings mag) and, up to that point at least, rambled on amiably about his domestic circumstances.

Home Truths showcased ordinary people's stories, and since Peel had sought to present himself as an ordinary person away from the 'day job' he was as qualified as anyone to become a quietly unobtrusive interrogator – and, more than once, a shoulder to cry on. He introduced the unbroadcast pilot programme thus: 'Saturdays, to some people, mean doing it yourself or getting out into the countryside and maybe killing something, or pretty much doing what you were doing the rest of the week, albeit after an extra thirty minutes in bed. To others it means a Saturday job, as it does from today to me.'

In fact, the show would be recorded on Thursdays, leaving Peel time to drive home and broadcast his Thursday-night Radio One offering from Peel Acres. It would prove a fair old workload for a diabetic who admitted to being 'tired and grumpy' in the afternoons, but he clearly found *Home Truths* uplifting when, on a Thursday morning, he'd sit and listen to the phone calls and readings selected for that week's programmes. 'Each week I arrive in our office on the eighth floor with my ample bosom heaving with optimism, a spring in my step, my eyes upturned towards the stars,' he wryly noted, 'certain that this week we will do great things together, effect some sort of moral advance to match the technological advances that threaten to engulf us all.'

Typically, Peel followed that chatty programme introduction with a downbeat pay-off line: 'And what do I find when I sit down, manly features aglow with moral purpose, to consider your letters, emails and text messages? Chickens and nail clippings, that's what I find.' However, despite the immense personal satisfaction he clearly derived from presenting *Home Truths*, he would reflect in 1999 that, with the programme barely a year old, he'd already taken 'more and harsher criticism than I've ever endured in my life, I must admit, some of it hurtful . . . It's been wild, unfocused and, in most cases, incredibly inaccurate.'

Much of this may have had something to do with the shifting of schedules (the shock of the new was something Radio Four aficionados, unlike those of Radio One, were definitely not used to). The newcomer's previous connections with the network had been a nervously delivered piece on the death in 1995 of the Grateful Dead's Jerry Garcia for *From Our Own Correspondent*, a more confident effort called *Offspring* – a half-hour weekly evening magazine programme about family life which aired at various times between 1995 and 1997 – and a cameo appearance on *The Archers*. Peel was a long-term fan of radio's longest-running soap, and was even a fully paid-up member of the Eddie Grundy Fan Club!

He endured the initial resistance to *Home Truths* and beat the critics by sticking with the job and making it his own. Bryan Gallagher, who appeared as a guest on the programme in 2001 and ended up writing for it, summed up Peel's gifts as 'a wonderful modesty, the ability to make people feel at their ease, to come into our living rooms and talk to us like a favourite uncle. I was constantly amazed by the range of his listening public; small farmers, captains of industry, lorry drivers, professional men all spoke to me about things that he had said.

'He was indeed a man for all seasons, who could walk with kings nor ever lose the common touch. In the last story that I wrote, I mentioned that I had once played in a small dance band, and he said, "I should like to hear a bit more about that." It is a bitter irony that I was sitting writing a story about the band, wondering if he would like it, when I was told the dreadful news [of his death].'

John would also have appreciated the following tribute from poet, pop star and writer Roger McGough, one-time member of fellow Merseysiders the Scaffold: 'Interviews can be tricky, especially with people who've never been on the radio before, and are perhaps talking about something quite personal. What John was able to do was put people at their ease, reassuring even the most nervous interviewee before the interview proper had even started. He was not a man who set out to dazzle guests with slick cross-examination techniques. "I'm not Jeremy Paxman," he would say, and that was certainly true.'

John Peel, the man who'd cured the homesickness of generations of painfully adolescent students, had returned to them as an agony uncle to see them through their problematic middle years. And while *Daily Telegraph* media critic Gillian Reynolds accused the BBC of cynicism – 'Let's get loads of people on with problems and get someone sensible to talk to them' – even she stopped well short of accusing our man of insincerity.

Having taken on and engaged Middle England, 2002 saw John Peel make a belated return to his roadshow days by playing a DJ set at Fabric, a London club that had bucked the trend as dance music went through a lull. It was his first club appearance for a decade, his last having been at Manchester's now closed but once ultra-trendy Haçienda. There, he'd been ignominiously 'stuck in some back room . . . People would occasionally stick their head round, then wander off looking very disappointed.'

Yet he'd clearly never given up hope of hitting the Wheels of Steel for one last time. 'When the offer came from Fabric, I mentioned it to the people at Radio One and they said it was a good idea. Mainly, I imagine, so they could get free tickets,' he said. Its success led to a request to compile one of Fabric's 'mix' CDs, which turned out to be another first: 'No one had asked me before; I'm afraid I'm not very ambitious.' In the end, he justified the exercise by saying it would be useful 'for people who've liked tunes I've played on the radio that are not easy to get hold of' – though with the tracks 'segueing' into one another, his trademark tones were not required: 'I'm not on it at all, except for the name.'

Three of the four Ravenscroft children had now graduated from university, something that brought problems of a different kind to those John had faced when they were younger: 'The distress you feel watching your grown-up kids trying to find decent work. One of my sons was treated so badly [by a boss], I said . . . I would go up to his office and detonate myself . . . the first white middle-class suicide bomber.'

It's doubtful he shared such murderous thoughts with members of the royal family when, in November, 1998, John went to Buckingham Palace to receive the Order of the British Empire. 'It's an interesting experience,' he told his *Home Truths* colleagues on air afterwards, likening the ceremony to 'going to a service in a church to which you don't belong'. He was disappointed that the children missed it – John's brothers accompanied him, along with the ever-present Pig – and even more sorry that his parents hadn't survived to see their son receive establishment recognition for his unconventional career. Sheila's father, who'd recently died, had been told about it before his passing: indeed, Peel's suit had had its first outing for his funeral. Its unusually sombre tones were now lightened by a tie in Liverpool FC red.

On this occasion, although the Palace had listed him as Peel, he preferred to use the family name: 'Today I wanted to be Ravenscroft.' Whether or not he cast his mind back to George VI, his childhood inspiration, is unrecorded.

Having earned his OBE, Peel would find himself receiving a more nebulous but arguably more meaningful honour as the new millennium started: he was voted forty-third in the BBC's national poll to find the all-time One Hundred Greatest Britons. 'It's quite clearly bollocks,' he scoffed, 'but in a way quite gratifying bollocks. When they invited me in for an interview about it, I suspected it was a piss-take. I thought someone would leap out and say, "You arrogant bastard."'

The latest accolade had to fight for its place on the Peel Acres mantelpiece alongside a plethora of radio gongs, including the 1993 Sony Award for Broadcaster of the Year, honorary degrees (seven, at last count) and, unforgettably, the Godlike Genius Award from *New Musical Express*, bestowed in 1994. The Radio Academy would induct him into its Hall of Fame in December 2003, where he joined such broadcasting greats as Richard Dimbleby, Alistair Cooke (who, sadly, would die in the same year as John) and . . . Tony Blackburn!

A clash with his one-time 'foe' had looked to be on the cards when, in 2002, Blackburn not only took part in but won the Australian-based TV reality show *I'm A Celebrity, Get Me Out Of Here!* Peel's ages-old description of him as an 'amiable buffoon' hardly ranked alongside the 'antichrist' label he'd also applied, but Blackburn's use of this to encourage viewers to vote for him inspired Peel to send him a low-key email of protest: 'I was very cross because I urged listeners to vote for him on that idiotic programme. The things he was saying that I'd said were from twenty years ago . . . He's a very strange man, but at the same time I have a grudging respect for him. He's remained true to what he believes in, in the same way I have.' Both then, however, and against all the odds in a youth-obsessed world, found themselves in greater demand than ever.

Not that Peel had countenanced any thoughts of retirement. In a late-1990 interview he'd considered the possibility of hanging up his stylus (or the digital equivalent) at the age of sixty-five and rejected it out of hand: 'I'm not the kind of bloke who thinks about retiring in fourteen years or whatever. There may come a time when I can't find any new records that I like – and I certainly couldn't fake it – but at the moment I relish people putting their heads round the door and saying "You call that music?" As you get older, you're supposed to drift into becoming more and more conservative, but I find myself becoming politically angrier with the passage of time. I'd rather have my hands cut off than vote Conservative.'

His political motivation had, however, been severely strained with the accession to power of Tony Blair and New Labour in 1997. Though Peel had briefly joined the touring circus accompanying Labour's election campaign, he would remark of the experience: 'I was on the bus, but I just sat there nervously looking out of the window. So I wasn't much use.' His old-style socialism had aligned him more with John Prescott, the bluff, no-nonsense ex-cruise liner steward who would rise to the heights of Deputy Prime Minister – albeit with a few gaffes and a famous bout of fisticuffs en route. So it was that Peel's disillusionment with New Labour would grow in the years preceding his death: he told Sophie Wilcockson in one of his last interviews that, after 'all that kowtowing to the Bush regime [over Iraq], I couldn't in all conscience vote for Labour now.'

If that made him a grumpy old man, then Peel was clearly going to make the most of his status. The year 2003 would see him once again tentatively re-enter the world of the gogglebox, buoyed by the company of such fellow fogeys as Bob Geldof, Will Self, Ken Stott and Rory McGrath, as one of the *Grumpy Old Men.* Friday nights were enlivened by TV discussions – or rather, diatribes – on such topics as body-piercing, crop tops and beer bellies, ponytails on men, tattoos, loud music in shops and text messaging, all features of modern times that riled the greying gents. Peel's observations were frequently hailed as among the most telling, and helped win him yet another tranche of fans for whom rock'n'roll was, now if not then, a closed book.

Yet to those who felt John Peel's tastemaking influence in matters musical was on the wane, his loyal listeners could use a terse two-word riposte: White Stripes. The curious garage-rock duo from Detroit followed Nirvana in receiving their first national radio exposure via Peel's good offices. The guitar and drums team of Jack and Meg White – some said brother and sister; others said husband and wife; they said little, further stoking the rumours – powered out a primeval sound greater than the sum of their parts that harked back to the blues in its rawest form. It was a recipe that certainly appealed to Peel, who would ensure that the summer of 2001 would introduce Great Britain to White Stripes fever.

'Each year I go to a town in the north of the Netherlands called Groningen,' he told the *New York Times* as it sought to explain the band's explosive impact from almost nothing. 'In Groningen, there's a great record shop. They'd got *White*

Blood Cells [the first White Stripes album] and it just looked so interesting, the concept of it. I bought it home, listened to it and started playing it on the radio. That sort of proper, over-the-top guitar playing – where you're actually playing something – has always been something I've enjoyed very much. So it was just good to hear that kind of guitar sound again.'

Other Peel 'finds' of the era included Roni Size, Hefner, Ladytron, the Yeah Yeah Yeahs and the Von Bondies. Some would remain cult listening, while others, such as Cerys Matthews's Catatonia, would graduate to the mainstream after accessing the airwaves via Peel.

Despite his Radio Four forays, his Radio One show was still delivering the goods for listeners across all generations. Little wonder, then, that, as he entered his fourth decade in UK broadcasting, John found himself in the happy position of having a higher percentage of listeners under sixteen listening to his Radio One programme than any other programme on the station – something he hazarded might *just* be a source of irritation to the more deliberately youth-orientated programming strands.

'We're not going to come close to the others in total number, obviously,' he quickly qualified, 'but percentage-wise I believe we do, which is quite nice. Because obviously I'm old enough to be their grandfather – and, as I always say rather flippantly, in the case of some of the ugly ones, very possibly am!'

10

Final Transmission

THE NEWS CAME THROUGH on a grey autumn Tuesday: John Peel had died of a heart attack in Peru. He had collapsed the previous evening while he and Sheila were visiting the ancient Inca city of Cuzco. Doctors at the Hotel Libertador, where the couple had arrived on the previous Saturday, tried to revive him after what was described as a 'massive' coronary, but he was pronounced dead at a local hospital. Reports suggested he'd suffered the fatal attack while having drinks with his wife at the Monasterio Hotel bar.

The planned two-week working holiday had enabled Peel to tour a country he had always wanted to visit. He was to return with the raw material for a travel feature for the *Daily Telegraph*, a tribute perhaps to the way he'd engaged the Radio Four audience via *Home Truths* after a rocky start. The trip had kicked off on 17 October and, having stayed in the Peruvian capital of Lima for two nights the Peels headed inland to Arequipa, in the picturesque Colca Canyon, and thence to Titicaca. They then caught a train to Cuzco, where they were scheduled to stay three nights before moving on to visit the Inca ruins at Machu Picchu. But it was not to be.

Peel had first ventured into print about his favourite holidays in May that year, among which were his honeymoon in Egypt – the pyramids had been 'one of the few sights I've seen that really exceeded my expectations' – and a stay the previous year in a château in the Dordogne with his family. Asked where he'd like to travel next, he'd said, 'South America, for new cultural experiences. But there's so much to see that it's rather daunting.' The *Telegraph* decided to grant his wish and the great man chose Peru as his destination: 'I've got a bad back and diabetes, and am not the most robust of travellers. But I'd like to see as much of the country as I can.'

It was a courageous choice for a man who admitted he had to take 'a prodigious amount of tranquillizers' to get through any flight. For this reason he chose an itinerary that kept the flying to a minimum once safely in South America, even if it meant subjecting his back to the variable quality of Peru's roads. His final question to the *Telegraph* travel desk had been, simply: 'Can I just double-check that you're happy to tell it as I see it?' Thus a 'colourful despatch' was awaited back in Blighty: instead, a call came on the Tuesday morning with the same bad news the country would learn just hours later; the only silver lining was that his beloved Pig had been there with him at the end.

Peel, who'd turned sixty-five just weeks earlier, would have been well advised to take it easy. Even the most athletic pensioner could find themselves short of breath in Cuzco, a place so high that flights there have to arrive in the early morning, before cloud cover sets in.

Andy Kershaw, twenty years Peel's junior, went public with claims that a fraught relationship between the DJ and BBC bosses could have been a factor in his recent ill health.

Kershaw told the *Daily Mirror* the veteran DJ had looked 'terrible' when he had last seen him three weeks previously. Peel had apparently said: 'They have put my programme back further into the night and I feel marginalized. It's killing me.'

In response to the claims, the BBC issued a strongly worded official statement, which read: 'Everyone at Radio One is shocked and upset by John's sudden death. When his family are still in deep mourning, and out of respect for them, this isn't the time to make these remarks or for us to comment on them.' An unnamed BBC executive supposedly went further: 'John was fully supportive of the changes – he even said the late finish meant clearer roads when he drove back to East Anglia.'

It had taken a considerable effort of will to go to Peru at all, given Peel's well-known aversion to flying, but he was prepared to surmount this challenge as 'Sheila doesn't get holidays and needs a treat'. He had also postponed another return date at Fabric, the London club where he was fast becoming a cult figure.

Novelist Andrew O'Hagan had accompanied Peel to New Zealand in 2002 on a venture that was not intended to produce a travelogue but saw the unlikely pair representing British culture – 'a fact that made us laugh for an entire week,' O'Hagan recalled. The writer formed an instant affinity with the DJ, not least because his youthful band the Big Gun had been one of countless short-lived local combos whose one and only single had been played on night-time radio by the great man. 'We then played a few gigs in the south and promptly split up,' O'Hagan later reflected. Yet he'd never forgotten the favour. 'To have the Peel seal of approval was, for several generations of bands and millions of listeners, like being inducted into the mysteries of some higher standard. We all believed in him because he seemed so pure.

Peel didn't sell music to you but, instead, exhibited a set of values and small humanities that could be imbibed by his audience every night for nothing.'

As ever, the trip had seen the DJ amass demo tapes and newfangled CD-Rs, pressed upon him by long-distance listeners who could now access him via the Internet: by the third day the number approached three figures, and, attentive as ever, he listened to them all while staying in a rented house with O'Hagan and the Pig. That appears to have been the last holiday he'd taken before tragedy struck.

Most serious newspapers printed predictably eulogistic obituaries, though the *Mail on Sunday* was quick to remind readers of Peel's unhappy first marriage. Running the curious headline 'Tragic end of the teen bride John Peel was accused of getting hooked on drugs' (the lawyers earned their money coming up with that one), they rehashed the story of tragic Shirley Anne Milburn, eliciting quotes from family and a subsequent husband. Its pay-off sentence, 'The tragedy was, that for all his sincerity and goodness, [Peel] never tried to rescue the young woman over whose life he cast such a fatal shadow,' seemed unforgivably harsh.

Coincidentally, the death had been announced the previous week of another pioneer whose lifetime mission had been to spread the gospel of rock'n'roll. American Greg Shaw, founder of the independent Bomp label, died of heart failure in Los Angeles aged fifty-five, his record company announced. Like Peel with the Fall and Captain Beefheart, Shaw had consistently championed artists regarded as too rough-and-ready for the music mainstream, the Stooges, the Germs and Seeds frontman Sky Saxon among them. Also like John, he had been a proponent of punk with groups such as the Flamin' Groovies, whom he managed – but when that term was appropriated to describe the Sex Pistols and their ilk, Shaw renamed it 'garage rock'. Shaw's record collection, which reputedly ran to seven figures, gave him something else in common with Peel.

It's perhaps a facile comparison to make, even given John's presence in the city of Dallas when President Kennedy was assassinated, but every Peel fan will forever remember where they were when they heard the news of his passing. Radio stations began playing 'Teenage Kicks' across the airwaves in tribute; Steve Wright's impromptu Radio Two medley was particularly touching. Millwall FC did the same before the following night's match against Liverpool in the third round of the League Cup, though the Reds stopped short of donning black armbands for one of their most famous supporters. Peel himself would have been heartened by the 3–0 victory for the Merseysiders, but saddened by the running battles between fans, allegedly ignited by tasteless Hillsborough-related chants. This particular kind of teenage kick would have taken John back to the horrors of the 1980s that had so affected him.

Peel had gone on broadcasting to the end, working from London on Tuesdays and Wednesdays, then broadcasting from his home studio on Thursdays (a fact, given that he did *Home Truths* on Thursday daytime, that makes the BBC's unattributed 'clearer roads' assertion ring less true). In 2003 he told *Record Collector* how much he enjoyed 'finishing the programme, taking the dogs for a walk and then going to bed'.

May 2004 had seen Morrissey, on the comeback trail, appear on Zane Lowe's show rather than Peel's programme due to what his label, Attack Records, described as a 'misunderstanding'. It seems the ex-Smiths singer 'wasn't listening' when they explained his session would be performed in front of a studio audience of twelve competition winners: he had been under the misapprehension that he would perform privately in a link to *The John Peel Show*. It echoed the experience of Morrissey's abortive first solo Peel session, which remained unheard after the singer pronounced the results unsatisfactory.

Other than this unexpected hiccup, everything seemed to be running smoothly in John Peel's life, even if the workload was unrelenting. He continued to prepare programmes at home for broadcast on the BBC's World Service (whose listeners he'd entertained for over two decades) and sundry strangely named European stations, obsessively ensuring the latter – comprising highlights from the week's shows on Radio One – never quite duplicated each other. On the lighter side, he'd just become a grandfather for the first time, to Archie, and was enjoying the occasional spot of 'vigorous grandparenting'.

Any spare time he had was taken up working on his autobiography, which was due to be delivered to the publishers in March 2005 and released the following Christmas. His advance, reputedly £1.5 million, was one of the biggest sums ever paid in Britain for such a book. It would undoubtedly have pleased Peel to have beaten Manchester United manager Sir Alex Ferguson, who signed for a 'mere' £1.2 million, while motor-racing commentator Murray Walker had settled for £1.4 million. By comparison, lesser lights such as former Spice Girl Geri Halliwell (£500,000) were left at the starting grid.

Only England football captain David Beckham, whose deal with HarperCollins amounted to £2 million, could boast a better haul. But while 'Goldenballs' had engaged former *EastEnders* actor Tom 'Lofty' Watt as his ghost-writer, Peel was to face the task of inputting the requisite 100,000 words alone. His agent, the *Daily Telegraph* reported, had circulated a synopsis outlining chapters about adolescent sexual encounters at Shrewsbury and rather more risky heterosexual affairs in America. The bidding war began at £1 million and, in just ten days, had attracted serious offers from half a dozen publishers.

Peel ended up choosing between Transworld, which offered £1.5 million, and HarperCollins, who offered 'slightly more'. Patrick Janson-Smith, joint managing director of Transworld, was confident Peel's memoirs would justify such an advance, reasoning his company could break even with hardback sales of 300,000–400,000 and similar paperback figures.

'John Peel is a much-loved and much-admired figure,' said Janson-Smith, 'and there is a real story there. As a DJ, he's been at the centre of the cultural scene since the 1960s and now he has a very strong appeal to Middle England through *Home Truths*. People absolutely love the programme.'

Shortly after Peel's passing, Transworld informed *New Musical Express* that they did not yet know whether the book would go ahead, and that his wife would be left to decide what happened with the title. 'It's tragic and we are all very shocked,' managing director Larry Finlay told the *Guardian*. 'It's just too early to know what will happen. John said in his radio broadcasts that he was regularly getting on with the writing, but a lot now will depend on what Sheila – to whom we send our deepest sympathies – wants.'

Finlay did not reveal how much of the book had actually been completed, but Peel reportedly confessed to the *Mirror* back in April that he had written just 1,500 out of the proposed 100,000 words. (Later estimates were higher, though Andy Kershaw said the eternally Luddite Peel had confessed to deleting 5,000 words at the touch of a wrong key.) He had, however, been forward-thinking enough to approach his first wife's family to request photographs of him in his mid-1960s Stateside heyday. 'He said he needed them for the new book, and assured us that he would say nothing in it to discredit Shirley Anne,' said Jan Milburn, wife of Shirley's brother Charles.

According to Sophie Wilcockson, whose interview for the University of Liverpool's alumni magazine *Insight* was published posthumously, Peel had admitted that, while he'd amassed 12,000 words, he had kept changing his approach to avoid a 'rather tedious' chronological approach. He kept 'whizzing backwards and forwards through time', while at the same time driving his long-suffering but computer-literate children mad by demanding constant 'technical support'.

Something else that might have proved a financial windfall was Peel's record collection – not that there had been a chance of him parting with it while he was still living and breathing. Yet, it would be revealed, he had already talked to the British Library with a view to bequeathing the collection to the nation. The National Sound Archive's curator, Andy Linehan, had paid a visit to Peel Acres to scrutinize it and declared it 'a fantastic collection. The nature of the material that was sent to him was the kind of stuff that we couldn't possibly get hold of.'

The National Sound Archive was understandably keen to lay claim to the collection (conservatively estimated at 26,000 LPs, 40,000 singles and 40,000 CDs by *New Musical Express*) to add to 2.5 million recordings already stored at the British Library building near London's King's Cross station. Yet while Clive Selwood was au fait with the discussions that took place prior to Peel's untimely death, he sounded a note of caution: 'The idea certainly had favour with him, but we'll just have to see what happens. It should stay in England, but I've got to look after the interests of the family. This was his great asset. He was never a great saver of money.' Selwood later revealed to the *Mirror* that an unnamed US radio company had offered 'over £1 million' for the 'priceless' collection.

With emotions and airplay running high, Peel's all-time favourite song was a possible contender for the coveted Christmas number-one slot. Bookies William Hill rated

Doing what he did best (*above*).

The Undertones (*below*) and Captain Beefheart (*inset, right*), just two of the acts John championed. The Undertones' 'Teenage Kicks' was John's favourite record of all time.

John's impact on the British music scene is immeasurable. He was always the first to play and promote emerging new sounds and brought countless acts and styles into the mainstream, including (*clockwise, from far left*) Bob Marley, Grandmaster Flash, Joy Division, The Smiths and the Sex Pistols.

Above: With fellow DJ Bob Harris at Radio Four in 1993. It was with this BBC radio station that Peel began broadcasting a new show, *Home Truths*, in 1998 – a programme which won him countless new fans. However, his first love remained new music: (*below*) John performs at Tribal Gathering in 1997.

Remarkably, John was still championing new acts well into his sixties. Britpop icon Jarvis Cocker (pictured with John in 2002, *right*) and the breakthrough group of 2004, the Scissor Sisters (*below*), were recent recipients of his support.

Radio's revolutionary DJ shares a joke with Princess Margaret at the *Desert Island Discs* fiftieth-birthday party in 1992 (*above*). Six years later, the Queen herself would honour Peel with an OBE (*left*).

Right: John collects an honorary degree from the University of East Anglia, one of several he received in his lifetime.

Below: With wife Sheila in 2002, receiving the radio industry's highest accolade, the Sony Gold Award, marking his outstanding contribution to radio in more than thirty-five years of broadcasting.

John Peel 1939–2004

'Teenage Kicks' the fourth favourite to take Yuletide honours in 2004, with odds of 14/1 before its release had even been confirmed. (John had always said he wanted 'Teenage dreams, so hard to beat' on his gravestone.)

Ironically, with a number-one single in 2004 achievable with just 21,000 sales, 'Teenage Kicks' would have been a shoo-in on fifty-one weeks of any given year. But the band's manager Andy Ferguson told reporters: 'It would be totally inappropriate to release "Teenage Kicks" as a single, and is not something the band would even consider.' Fans of the song instead had to make do with a live cover version by Snow Patrol, recorded at the South By Southwest festival in Texas earlier in 2004. They made the recording available for free download as a 'gift in memory of John Peel' and stated on their website that although they 'never had the honour of a Peel session or meeting him' they 'greatly admired' the DJ, adding: 'He was responsible for saving Radio One from chart hell and he will be sorely missed.'

A more credible tribute was announced by Glastonbury's Michael Eavis with the news that the new bands stage at his annual festival was to be renamed in Peel's honour. 'It's very appropriate,' said rock'n'roll's favourite farmer, 'because it's all the sort of music that John would have chosen.' The Undertones immediately contacted Eavis to book their place on the stage. 'As soon as they found out about the John Peel Stage they were on the phone asking if they could play,' he reported, 'because John helped make them too.'

John Peel's funeral was delayed until mid-November since, as with all deaths abroad, there were logistical hurdles to be surmounted and considerable red tape to be cut through before his body could be repatriated. Fans were delighted to learn they'd be able to pay their own final respects with the service at St Edmundsbury Cathedral in Bury St Edmunds on Friday 12 November open to all. As is usual in these circumstance, the public farewell would be followed by a private service for family and friends.

Hundreds of fans and well-wishers, unable to join John's close family and celebrity mourners such as Jarvis Cocker, Feargal Sharkey and Robert Plant inside the church, stood quietly outside as a clear, sunny morning gave way to grey and drizzle. Alongside such traditional fare as 'Abide With Me', the service included Howlin' Wolf's 'Going Down Slow' and Roy Orbison's 'Running Scared'. Scripture readings came from Clive Selwood and the BBC's Chris Lycett, while tributes were read by Paul Gambaccini, John's brother Alan, and Charlie Bell, a family friend, who read out some amusing memories on behalf of the Ravenscroft children.

After the blessing, the unmistakable strains of Grinderswitch's 'Pickin' The Blues' suddenly and eerily punctured the silence. For a few minutes, it was as if John was speaking from beyond the grave as, one final time, that familiar, sardonic voice filled the mourners' ears with a few choice previously broadcast anecdotes.

And still it wasn't quite over. The swell of the Kop Choir singing 'You'll Never Walk Alone' began to fade, giving way to an unmistakable, almost inevitable guitar riff. As the coffin left the cathedral to the strains of the Undertones' 'Teenage Kicks', the sombre mood evaporated and the people outside sang along and applauded. A suitable way to bid farewell to a man of the people.

★

Fittingly, it was the Fall who came top of the final, posthumous Festive Fifty with their 'Theme From Sparta F.C. Part 2', when Rob da Bank, the man with the thankless task of filling Peel's shoes on the late-night Radio One weekday slot, counted down the chart over the Christmas period. Hard though it is to believe, the Fall had topped the Festive Fifty only once before, in 1990 with 'Bill Is Dead', while the original 'Theme From Sparta F.C.' had been number two in the previous year's poll.

Radio One paid its own tribute to Peel on 16 December when it turned over its evening schedule to Steve Lamacq and friends. Underworld, the Wedding Present and Steveless were among the acts performing at Maida Vale from 8 to 11.30 p.m. after an early-evening documentary had opened proceedings: the night finished with a final ninety minutes featuring DJs Dynamite AC, Alex Patterson, Dave Clarke, Hixxy and Coldcut.

When asked to select a song to be played as part of the evening, John's widow Sheila chose 'Does This Train Stop On Merseyside?' by Liverpool band Amsterdam. 'At first I said no when I was asked,' she revealed, 'because I'm not very good at that sort of thing. John just really loved the Amsterdam song. He always became really emotional when he played it. He wasn't capable of playing it without crying. If he played it on the radio, he'd have to put something else on immediately afterwards because he wouldn't be able to speak. And when he played it at home, he'd always need a cuddle afterwards.'

Talking to the *Liverpool Echo*, she further revealed that the Ravenscroft family had been 'enormously touched' by the tributes to her late husband. 'So many people have been so enormously kind,' she told the paper, adding that John would have been 'beside himself' had he known about public reaction to his death.

The new year of 2005 saw Radio One decide that the gap left by the irreplaceable DJ was too great for one person to fill. Thus a different presenter each night would host a new show called OneMusic, which claimed to maintain Peel's passion for 'diverse, unpredictable and non-commercial' new music.

As the three presenters, Huw Stephens (Tuesdays), Ras Kwame (Wednesdays) and Rob da Bank (Thursdays), kicked off on 1 February, Radio One boss Andy Parfitt told reporters: 'As a DJ, John Peel was unique. Supporting new music and seeking out the unusual was at the heart of what John was about. We have spent a long time debating how best to continue John's work, and believe that, by having a series of DJs hosting a selection of shows under the OneMusic title, we will ensure that his legacy lives on.'

There have been many tributes to John Peel, and it is to be hoped that there will be several permanent memorials. Perhaps the site of the now demolished Egton House, where he was billeted for so many years, or in front of Broadcasting House might be appropriate places. Certainly, the Beatles statue in Liverpool's Mathew Street, by the former site of the Cavern Club, could use some competition from the man who, lest it be forgotten, first made his name partly through their reflected glory, at several thousand miles' distance.

In the city of Liverpool, on the day after John's death was announced, former Crowded House brothers Neil and Tim Finn graced the same Empire stage on which Peel saw Eddie Cochran perform back in 1960. He surely would have approved of Smiths' guitarist Johnny Marr joining them to play harmonica on the Crowded House hit 'Four Seasons In One Day'. Then, as if prompted by a shout from the stalls, Marr strapped on a guitar and the assembled band burst into 'Teenage Kicks' in an impromptu tribute. The icing on the cake came with a version of Smiths' classic 'There Is A Light That Never Goes Out' – a sentiment entirely appropriate to Peel's life and example.

May his pioneering spirit never be extinguished.

Tributes

'John's influence has towered over the development of popular music for nearly four decades and his contribution to modern music and music culture is immeasurable.'
ANDY PARFITT, Controller of Radio One

'He was a very funny, very warm man and we will always be grateful for what he did for the Undertones. He always had his finger on the pulse of the music industry and the fact that Radio One played the Undertones, the White Stripes and the Strokes today showed just how relevant he remained throughout his career.'
MICHAEL BRADLEY, Undertones

'John was a great Liverpudlian guy who I respected for his integrity and his love of non-mainstream music, which he successfully championed and brought to a large audience. He will be missed by a lot of people, including me.'
SIR PAUL McCARTNEY

'I was fortunate enough to meet him and play a session at his home. I remember we had a great conversation about Elvis that day. He was the first to play our debut single "Caught By The Fuzz" on radio, which I know brought us to people's attention. He was a big influence to so many.'
GAZ COOMBES, Supergrass

'He was utterly sincere in what he was doing, not because he wanted to be famous, but he thought he was on a mission to bring stuff to people's ears. He really did trawl through mailbags of demo cassettes. That's why we had Pulp and T. Rex, because he'd been discovering bands like that since 1967.'
LIZ KERSHAW, former Radio One DJ

'In the early days of Zeppelin he gave us radio airplay when we were considered taboo by the flaccid BBC identikit disc jockeys.'
ROBERT PLANT, Led Zeppelin

'I dedicate that song to an absent friend, Mr John Peel. Actually, he never liked the Divine Comedy, but he knew what he liked, he stuck to it and he never wavered. Here's a Joy Division song, especially for him . . .'
NEIL HANNON, Divine Comedy,
on stage at the Royal Albert Hall

'I heard on the plane to San Francisco and I cried. He was the first person that ever played Hole in Britain. He was magical. He was a wizard. He got people right at the right moment. We dedicated our show [in San Francisco] to him and I cried.'
COURTNEY LOVE, Hole

'John was the single most important broadcaster we have ever known. In the autumn of 1978, something happened that was to change my life for ever – John Peel played "Teenage Kicks" on the radio for the very first time.'
FEARGAL SHARKEY, former frontman of the Undertones

'The Prime Minister was genuinely saddened by the news . . . His view is John Peel was a genuine one-off, whether on Radio One or Radio Four. He was a unique voice in British broadcasting, and used that voice to unearth new talent and different subjects and make them accessible to a much wider audience.'
TONY BLAIR's official spokesman

'No more Festive Fifties, no more Peel sessions, no more records played at the wrong speed. He seemed like he'd always be there. He was my favourite DJ of all time by miles, and a really warm, lovely man.'
CARL BARÂT, Libertines

'He was one of those few people about whom you could truly say that the world would have been a much different place without him. In a world that is becoming ever more homogenized and pre-programmed, John Peel stuck up for the "sore thumbs" of the music scene.'
JARVIS COCKER, Pulp

'He is more important than any artist because he was the enthusiast who discovered so many of those whom we think of as the big figures of pop over the past forty years. John Peel was the most important figure in British music since the birth of rock'n'roll. Full stop.'
ANDY KERSHAW, fellow BBC radio presenter

'Very simply, John Peel made the world, and the world of music, a better place.'
MOBY

'Peel was the first person to put us on the radio – we sent him a demo and he became a patron to New Order and Joy Division. His was the only show that you could be satisfied by and infuriated by within the same hour. He was immune to fashion, he just liked what he liked. That's why people loved him – he took chances, and people these days very rarely take chances.'
PETER HOOK, Joy Division/New Order

'He was dry, sardonic, laid-back, modest, even shy, but very passionate. He wasn't anything like a celebrity, and was as far removed from group market research or focus groups as you can get.'
DAVID 'KID' JENSEN,
DJ and former *Top of the Pops* co-host

'He was the only guy on commercial nationwide radio that played Australian drill'n'bass at half past ten in the evening.

I don't know where else we're going to hear stuff like that now.
I remember being really excited when we went to do our
first Peel session.'
ROSS MILARD, Futureheads

'He qualifies as probably the most important single figure in the
British music industry for the last forty-eight years.'
BRIAN ENO

'A lot of people – me included – feel like we've lost our surrogate
dad. John was the first person to play one of my band's records
when I was sixteen; because of him I got a record deal, and my
first really serious TV job was presenting Glastonbury alongside
him and Jo Whiley. Now I'm a DJ on XFM – a whole radio
station built around John's kind of show. I feel stupid for being
as in debt as I am.'
LAUREN LAVERNE, Kenickie

'In the States, there is absolutely no one who compares to him,
and if some radio DJ did get courageous enough to play whatever
bands he or she wanted to, strictly on the merit of musical quality,
he'd quickly find his ass out on the street with no job. Consider
yourselves lucky to have had this guiding force in your world.'
GRANDADDY

'I just can't believe it. You never thought John Peel was going to
die. He made an incredible contribution to British music. When
I arrived at Radio One, he took me under his wing. He was
totally passionate. He was passionate about football and music.
More, he was passionate about his family.'
JANICE LONG, former Radio One DJ

'He had an open mind about music, whether he was bringing the
listener the Incredible String Band or the Fall, Mike Hart or Echo
and the Bunnymen, and countless bands that appeared only to be

heard on his great shows. He was a great man, a fabulous curmudgeon, and he was as rare as the music that he loved.'
ELVIS COSTELLO

'When I was thirteen I was in a terrible punk band and sent him a terrible record, and he played it a couple of times on his show. I remember it being one of the most amazing moments in my life.'
SAM HELIHY, Hope of the States

'I used to listen to him loads as a kid. He had a way of flipping you so you ended up liking things you wouldn't normally have given any attention. He messed with my blinkers so much they fell off after a bit. Without him being around we probably wouldn't have bothered making music at all. Radio One was basically a dead zone to us except for occasional jolts, but his show was totally solid; end-to-end what he wanted to play – nothing brought his playlist together other than the fact that he liked it. It's a rare thing these days for anyone at all to rely only on their gut and just feel something. He's responsible for so much . . . I can't imagine the world without him.'
SEAN BOOTH, Autechre

'I think he might be the greatest comedian of his era. Someone like Jack Dee has taken the John Peel persona – that morose, dry, grouchy character – and made it his art. But Peel played life-changing records between his patter.'
CHARLIE GILLETT, author and broadcaster

'He championed Welsh-language music and for years was the only DJ on national radio who was willing to embrace it. He was very wary of trends such as Britpop. He was introducing people to drum'n'bass and techno, things that were going on outside of the media.'
GRUFF RHYS, Super Furry Animals

'He was groundbreaking for me. He just broke the rules the whole time. He did things that just weren't done. He was a maverick and he got away with it. You have to have trust with a DJ, and everyone built that trust with John.'
STEVE LAMACQ, Radio One DJ

'John Peel's patronage was for me, like countless other musicians, one of the most significant things that happened to us in our careers. The world is going to be a poorer place with his sudden departure.'
DAMON ALBARN, Blur

'He was one of the only DJs who championed music. I hope [his death] will shame Radio One and other DJs into taking a more constructive role.'
PETE SHELLEY, Buzzcocks

'He had an indelible passion for music. He wasn't in it for the fame, he wasn't in it for his own career – he was in it because he genuinely believed in sharing the music he found exciting with an audience.'
MATTHEW BANNISTER, former Radio One Controller

'John was simply one of my favourite men in the whole world; as a music fan and presenter he was simply an inspiration.'
JO WHILEY, Radio One DJ
and co-presenter of *Glastonbury Live*

'Whenever I was losing inspiration, I would listen to the show and was straight away on track. He'd play one thing every show which would change how you thought about a style of music. I don't know how he managed to keep doing that and have that burning enthusiasm.'
THOM YORKE, Radiohead

'John's dry, quintessentially English voice led me and millions of others into an esoteric world of music, full of imagination and adventure. There was a curious contrast between the matter-of-fact homeliness of Peel's presentation and the wild eclecticism of his musical taste. Yet he was the ideal host to the most arcane portals of pop culture precisely because he never made them seem challenging and uninviting.'
NEIL McCORMICK, *Daily Telegraph* rock critic

'John Peel was a unique broadcaster whose influence on Radio One could be felt from its very first days. He nurtured musicians and listeners alike, introducing them to new sounds. His open-minded approach to music was mirrored by his equally generous approach to his audience when he went to Radio Four to present *Home Truths*.'
JENNY ABRAMSKY, BBC Director of Radio and Music

'It was always great to listen to John. He was a crucial figure for music and he often thought that the BBC were trying to sideline him. The station went through various controllers who were not always keen on having an individual, distinctive voice, which John Peel was.'
ALEXEI SAYLE, comedian

'If it wasn't for John Peel, there would be no Joy Division and no New Order. He was one of the few people to give bands that played alternative music a chance to get heard, and he continued to be a champion of cutting-edge music.'
BERNARD SUMNER, Joy Division/New Order

'He had pretenders behind him, but while they all moved into specializing he never did that – which was the secret of new music. It's a tragedy because we're living in a very homogenized world.'
BEE STOREY, Clive Selwood's daughter

'He was an avid supporter, and was very passionate about football. I met him once and he talked about nothing else but the team. Liverpool people are proud people and we feel connected to those who go on to become famous. He will be missed.'
TOMMY SMITH, Liverpool FC

'He was a true original, but he had the thing that every great broadcaster has in that he was completely genuine. What you got over talking to him in an Indian restaurant was the same John Peel you'd hear on the radio.'
TREVOR DANN, former Peel producer

'We were headlining one night at the 2002 Sonar Festival in Barcelona and, somewhat to our surprise, his producer came to see us backstage to say that John Peel wondered if we would like to record a session for his show. It felt like an unexpected honour and so, later that year, we recorded four songs in the BBC Maida Vale studios. When he played them he remarked that any listeners surprised to be hearing the Pet Shop Boys on his show could just pretend they were listening to an obscure German electronic group. I always respected the way he dug out music that would be unheard elsewhere on Radio One.'
NEIL TENNANT, Pet Shop Boys

'For forty years he listened to music at home, at work and in the car. I honestly think it is quite likely that John Peel is the human being who has heard the most musical selections in the history of the world. He certainly kept humble about it.'
PAUL GAMBACCINI, former Radio One DJ

'Meeting him in the 1970s was a delight: he was just as cool, wise, sardonic and self-deprecating as he seemed on radio, even retaining good humour when he overnighted at my flat and got his feet sprayed by my un-neutered tomcat. Though I rarely listened to his show in the past few years, it was a comfort to

know that it, and he, were still there. I cannot imagine anyone else currently on UK music radio being able to match his unique combination of taste and dedication. John Peel will prove irreplaceable.'
CHARLES SHAAR MURRAY, music writer

'Before I was in a band he gave me so much music. When we were teenagers we'd stay up listening to his show and taping things from it, and I'd go to a friend, "Listen to this, it's really weird," and it would be something like "O Superman" by Laurie Anderson, which of course went on to become a legendary record. Peel introduced me to "Blue Monday" by New Order, that bass drum riff and using a drum machine in that fashion. Without hearing that, who knows . . . ? He is irreplaceable, not least because Radio One wouldn't give someone like Peel a job now. He survived every trend and every cull, a total one-off, and was more cutting-edge at the age of sixty-five than any DJ there.'
PAUL HARTNOLL, Orbital

'Who else could be mistaken for a Beatle in America [because of his accent] and knew Marc Bolan when he was still practising in his garage? Without John, I don't think Rough Trade would have been able to grow and support the artists we have. Most of our bands did their first radio session with him: the Fall, the Blue Orchids, the Smiths. Think of people like Mark E. Smith and Ivor Cutler, who would probably have been consigned to the dustbin of history without him: these are some of the geniuses of our culture. Also, giving Jarvis Cocker a session when he was still a schoolboy changed the course of his life. I'm sure it's the same for thousands of other artists.'
GEOFF TRAVIS, Rough Trade Records

'In 1985 we went and stood outside the BBC with the first record we made, 'cause he often said he played records given to him outside. I think we were there for four hours because we hadn't

worked out what time he arrived. [When he eventually came out] he said, "This any good?" and we said, "Yes." We listened every night until he played it, but we would have anyway. John Peel was our universe for a long time.'
KEVIN SHIELDS, My Bloody Valentine

'You can't overestimate the power of hearing your song being played by John Peel. He supported just about everything our label put out, even when no one else was interested. My mum doesn't even like this music – but having it played on Radio One validates it. Getting played on his show is what keeps indie labels going, and I don't know where that is going to come from now. No one else could have taste that catholic without being fake.'
PAUL SAVAGE, Delgados and co-founder of Chemikal Underground Records

'We once did a Peel session and instead of the usual four songs of three minutes we did a twelve-minute song, which was the antithesis of everything the Peel show was about: short, punky, unpretentious. A rumour reached us that he wasn't pleased – but fair play to him, he played it twice. I would like to think he thought, "What a bunch of chancers" and had a good laugh. He was always incredibly personable, just like some bloke you'd meet down the road.'
COLIN NEWMAN, Wire

'I spent ten or fifteen years listening to Peel – everything I love as a music-listener came from him. It was a dream come true for us to get played on his show, let alone to get asked to do a session. We were supposed to be recording that next week. It's possible that we're one of the last bands to benefit from his patronage. It's going to be much more of a struggle for bands to get played on the radio now.'
GORDON MOAKES, Bloc Party

John Peel's Festive Fifties

Each and every November, John Peel would devote himself to 'three or four weeks of serious tedium' by encouraging his Radio One listeners to nominate their favourite tracks of the past year.

In those pre-computerized days, he'd enter their votes in a ledger – with over 5,000 responses, this was no easy task – and, at the end of this 'proto-Dickensian routine', would emerge with the Festive Fifty.

He'd regularly complain that the listeners failed to keep up with the times (for which read his tastes), resulting in a chart that was 'conservative and nostalgic' – though one of the more adventurous notions that one listener proposed was to list the top fifty tracks but broadcast numbers fifty-one to one hundred. 'Not a bad idea at all,' chuckled the master of mayhem.

If nothing else, the Festive Fifty gives some idea of the changing face of music as broadcast by Peel over nearly thirty years.

Festive Fifty 1976

1 Led Zeppelin – Stairway To Heaven
2 Derek and the Dominoes – Layla
3 Bob Dylan – Desolation Row
4 Pink Floyd – Echoes
5 Jimi Hendrix – All Along The Watchtower
6 Free – All Right Now
7 Racing Cars – They Shoot Horses Don't They?
8 Pink Floyd – Shine On You Crazy Diamond
9 Beatles – A Day In The Life
10 Bob Dylan – Like A Rolling Stone
11 Poco – Rose Of Cimarron
12 Neil Young – Cortez The Killer
13 Rolling Stones – Brown Sugar
14 Beatles – Hey Jude
15 Legendary Stardust Cowboy – Paralysed
16 Jimi Hendrix – Voodoo Chile
17 Beatles – Strawberry Fields Forever
18 Captain Beefheart – Big Eyed Beans From Venus
19 Led Zeppelin – Whole Lotta Love
20 Lynyrd Skynyrd – Free Bird
21 Van Morrison – Madame George
22 Doors – Riders On The Storm
23 Bob Dylan – Visions Of Johanna
24 Jefferson Airplane – White Rabbit
25 Deep Purple – Child In Time
26 Little Feat – Long Distance Love
27 Grinderswitch – Pickin' The Blues
28 Joe Walsh – Rocky Mountain Way
29 Who – Won't Get Fooled Again
30 Misunderstood – I Can Take You To The Sun
31 Genesis – Supper's Ready
32 Bob Marley and the Wailers – No Woman, No Cry
33 Jonathan Richman – Roadrunner
34 Rod Stewart – Maggie May
35 Jackson Browne – Late For The Sky
36 Led Zeppelin – Kashmir
37 Jimi Hendrix – Hey Joe
38 Allman Brothers Band – Jessica
39 Rolling Stones – Jumpin' Jack Flash
40 Grateful Dead – Dark Star
41 Richard Thompson – I Want To See The Bright Lights Tonight
42 Family – The Weaver's Answer
43 Jackson Browne – Fountain Of Sorrow
44 Bob Dylan – Hurricane
45 Doors – Light My Fire
46 Matching Mole – O Caroline
47 Roy Harper – When An Old Cricketer Leaves The Crease
48 Wild Man Fischer – Go To Rhino Records
49 Little Feat – Willin'
50 Yes – And You And I

John Peel's Festive Fifties

Festive Fifty 1977

It is believed that because of various family matters that cropped up throughout the year, John Peel had to spend quite some time away from the programme, and was unable to host the Festive Fifty as normal in 1977. He did manage to compile his own list of favourite tracks of the year, however, of which the Top Thirteen have been salvaged and are reproduced below.

1 Motors – Dancing The Night Away
2 Althea and Donna – Uptown Top Ranking
3 Motors – You Beat The Hell Out Of Me
4 Rezillos – Can't Stand My Baby
5 John Cooper Clarke – Suspended Sentence
6 Desperate Bycycles – Smokescreen
7 Merelene Webber – Right Track
8 Neil Young – Like A Hurricane
9 Clash – Complete Control
10 Frankie Miller – Be Good To Yourself
11 Sex Pistols – Holidays In The Sun
12 Lurkers – Shadow
13 Jah Hayes/Ranking Trevor – Truly

Festive Fifty 1978

1 Sex Pistols – Anarchy In The UK
2 Clash – Complete Control
3 Sex Pistols – God Save The Queen
4 Stiff Little Fingers – Suspect Device
5 Magazine – Shot By Both Sides
6 Sex Pistols – Pretty Vacant
7 Clash – White Man In Hammersmith Palais
8 Buzzcocks – What Do I Get?
9 Public Image Ltd – Public Image
10 Undertones – Teenage Kicks
11 Stiff Little Fingers – Alternative Ulster
12 Buzzcocks – Boredom
13 Damned – New Rose
14 Led Zeppelin – Stairway To Heaven
15 Clash – White Riot
16 David Bowie – Heroes
17 Only Ones – Another Girl, Another Planet
18 Sex Pistols – Holidays In The Sun
19 Lynyrd Skynyrd – Free Bird
20 Rezillos – I Can't Stand My Baby
21 Van Morrison – Madame George
22 Siouxsie and the Banshees – Hong Kong Garden
23 Clash – Police And Thieves
24 Jam – Down In The Tube Station At Midnight
25 Elvis Costello – Watching The Detectives
26 Bruce Springsteen – Born To Run

27 Ian Dury and the Blockheads – Sex And Drugs And Rock And Roll

28 Dire Straits – Sultans Of Swing

29 Pink Floyd – Shine On You Crazy Diamond

30 Buzzcocks – Moving Away From The Pulsebeat

31 Derek and the Dominoes – Layla

32 Stranglers – Hanging Around

33 Stranglers – No More Heroes

34 Siouxsie and the Banshees – Helter Skelter

35 Motors – Dancing The Night Away

36 Bob Dylan – Like A Rolling Stone

37 Elvis Costello – Alison

38 Siouxsie and the Banshees – Overground

39 Who – My Generation

40 Stranglers – London Lady

41 Siouxsie and the Banshees – Switch

42 Siouxsie and the Banshees – Mirage

43 Siouxsie and the Banshees – Jigsaw Feeling

44 Jam – In The City

45 Sex Pistols – EMI

46 Bob Dylan – Desolation Row

47 Flying Lizards – Summertime Blues

48 Neil Young – Like A Hurricane

49 Thin Lizzy – Emerald

50 Siouxsie and the Banshees – Metal Postcard

Festive Fifty 1979

1 Sex Pistols – Anarchy In The UK

2 Undertones – Teenage Kicks

3 Clash – White Man In Hammersmith Palais

4 Jam – Down In The Tube Station At Midnight

5 Clash – Complete Control

6 Stiff Little Fingers – Alternative Ulster

7 Special AKA – Gangsters

8 Stiff Little Fingers – Suspect Device

9 Public Image Ltd – Public Image

10 Damned – New Rose

11 Ruts – In A Rut

12 Undertones – Get Over You

13 Sex Pistols – God Save The Queen

14 Sex Pistols – Holidays In The Sun

15 Stiff Little Fingers – Johnny Was

16 Sex Pistols – Pretty Vacant

17 Magazine – Shot By Both Sides

18 Stiff Little Fingers – Wasted Life

19 Jam – Eton Rifles

20 Only Ones – Another Girl, Another Planet

21 Siouxsie and the Banshees – Love In A Void

22 Damned – Love Song

23 Gang of Four – Damaged Goods

24 Led Zeppelin – Stairway To Heaven

25 Buzzcocks – Boredom

26 Clash – White Riot

27 Jam – Strange Town

28 Public Image Ltd – Death Disco

29 Undertones – You've Got My Number

30 Pink Floyd – Shine On You Crazy Diamond
31 Undertones – Jimmy Jimmy
32 Who – My Generation
33 Dead Kennedys – California Über Alles
34 David Bowie – Heroes
35 Siouxsie and the Banshees – Icon
36 Specials – Too Much Too Young
37 Skids – Into The Valley
38 Siouxsie and the Banshees – Switch
39 Tubeway Army – Are Friends Electric?
40 Fall – Rowche Rumble
41 Mekons – Where Were You?
42 Siouxsie and the Banshees – Jigsaw Feeling
43 Cure – 10:15 Saturday Night
44 Siouxsie and the Banshees – Playground Twist
45 Stranglers – No More Heroes
46 Siouxsie and the Banshees – Helter Skelter
47 Ruts – Babylon's Burning
48 Siouxsie and the Banshees – Hong Kong Garden
49 Clash – Police And Thieves
50 Buzzcocks – What Do I Get?

Festive Fifty 1980

(a year in which a longer list was produced . . .)

1 Sex Pistols – Anarchy In The UK
2 Joy Division – Atmosphere
3 Joy Division – Love Will Tear Us Apart
4 Jam – Down In The Tube Station At Midnight
5 Clash – White Man In Hammersmith Palais
6 Dead Kennedys – Holiday In Cambodia
7 Undertones – Teenage Kicks
8 Damned – New Rose
9 Stiff Little Fingers – Alternative Ulster
10 Joy Division – Transmission
11 Public Image Ltd – Public Image
12 Sex Pistols – Holidays In The Sun
13 Jam – Going Underground
14 Joy Division – Decades
15 Clash – Complete Control
16 Stiff Little Fingers – Johnny Was
17 Undertones – Get Over You
18 Cure – A Forest
19 Ruts – In A Rut
20 Joy Division – New Dawn Fades
21 Fall – Totally Wired
22 Joy Division – She's Lost Control
23 Sex Pistols – Pretty Vacant
24 Stiff Little Fingers – Suspect Device
25 Sex Pistols – God Save The Queen
26 Fall – How I Wrote Elastic Man
27 Stiff Little Fingers – Wasted Life
28 Only Ones – Another Girl, Another Planet
29 Damned – Love Song
30 Adam and the Ants – Kings Of The Wild Frontier
31 Dead Kennedys – California Über Alles
32 Special AKA – Gangsters
33 Public Image Ltd – Poptones
34 Public Image Ltd – Careering
35 Killing Joke – Requiem

36 Killing Joke – Psyche

37 Siouxsie and the Banshees – Jigsaw Feeling

38 Fall – Fiery Jack

39 Clash – Armagideon Time

40 Spizz Energi – Where's Captain Kirk?

41 Joy Division – Twenty-Four Hours

42 Damned – Smash It Up

43 Teardrop Explodes – Treason

44 Siouxsie and the Banshees – Switch

45 Siouxsie and the Banshees – Icon

46 Clash – Bank Robber

47 Siouxsie and the Banshees – Hong Kong Garden

48 Clash – White Riot

49 Fall – Rowche Rumble

50 Gang of Four – Damaged Goods

51 Siouxsie and the Banshees – Love In A Void

52 Killing Joke – Wardance

53 Adam and the Ants – Dog Eat Dog

54 Ruts – West One (Shine On Me)

55 Who – My Generation

56 Mo-Dettes – White Mice

57 Stiff Little Fingers – Tin Soldiers

58 Stranglers – No More Heroes

59 Jam – Eton Rifles

60 Pink Floyd – Shine On You Crazy Diamond

61 Magazine – Shot By Both Sides

62 Public Image Ltd – Death Disco

63 Led Zeppelin – Stairway To Heaven

64 Joy Division – Dead Souls

65 Wah! Heat – Better Scream

Festive Fifty 1981

(a longer list was produced for the second year running)

1 Joy Division – Atmosphere

2 Sex Pistols – Anarchy In The UK

3 Joy Division – Love Will Tear Us Apart

4 New Order – Ceremony

5 Joy Division – New Dawn Fades

6 Undertones – Teenage Kicks

7 Joy Division – Decades

8 Cure – A Forest

9 Dead Kennedys – Holiday In Cambodia

10 Clash – White Man In Hammersmith Palais

11 Joy Division – Dead Souls

12 Damned – New Rose

13 Jam – Down In The Tube Station At Midnight

14 Joy Division – Transmission

15 Altered Images – Dead Pop Stars

16 Stiff Little Fingers – Alternative Ulster

17 Sex Pistols – Holidays In The Sun

18 Clash – Complete Control

19 Birthday Party – Release The Bats

20 Undertones – Get Over You

21 Specials – Ghost Town

22 Scritti Politti – The Sweetest Girl

23 Jam – Going Underground

24 Stiff Little Fingers – Johnny Was

25 Theatre of Hate – Legion

26 Public Image Ltd – Public Image

27 Killing Joke – Requiem

28 Killing Joke – Follow The Leaders

29 Heaven 17 – We Don't Need This Fascist Groove Thang
30 Fall – Fiery Jack
31 Ruts – In A Rut
32 Stiff Little Fingers – Suspect Device
33 Fall – How I Wrote Elastic Man
34 Laurie Anderson – O Superman
35 Siouxsie and the Banshees – Jigsaw Feeling
36 B-Movie – Remembrance Day
37 Siouxsie and the Banshees – Israel
38 Sex Pistols – God Save The Queen
39 Pigbag – Papa's Got A Brand-New Pigbag
40 Siouxsie and the Banshees – Icon
41 Only Ones – Another Girl, Another Planet
42 Dead Kennedys – California Über Alles
43 Joy Division – Twenty-Four Hours
44 Joy Division – Isolation
45 Killing Joke – Psyche
46 Echo and the Bunnymen – Over The Wall
47 Fall – Lie Dream Of A Casino Soul
48 New Order – Procession
49 Siouxsie and the Banshees – Switch
50 Altered Images – Happy Birthday
51 Joy Division – She's Lost Control
52 Bauhaus – Bela Lugosi's Dead
53 Magazine – Shot By Both Sides
54 New Order – In A Lonely Place

55 Anti-Pasti – No Government
56 Fall – Totally Wired
57 Special AKA – Gangsters
58 Fire Engines – Candyskin
59 Sex Pistols – Pretty Vacant
60 Siouxsie and the Banshees – Hong Kong Garden

Festive Fifty 1982

(Part 1 – the year's favourites)

1 New Order – Temptation
2 Robert Wyatt – Shipbuilding
3 Grandmaster Flash and the Furious 5 – The Message
4 Echo and the Bunnymen – The Back Of Love
5 Tears For Fears – Mad World
6 Clash – Straight To Hell
7 Wah! Heat – The Story Of The Blues
8 Theatre of Hate – Do You Believe In The Westworld?
9 Artery – Into The Garden
10 Wild Swans – Revolutionary Spirit
11 Jam – Town Called Malice
12 Yazoo – Only You
13 Scritti Politti – Faithless
14 Associates – Party Fears Two
15 Bauhaus – Ziggy Stardust
16 Siouxsie and the Banshees – Fireworks
17 New Order – Hurt
18 Scritti Politti – Asylums In Jerusalem
19 Dexy's Midnight Runners – Come On Eileen
20 Killing Joke – Empire Song
21 Farmer's Boys – Whatever Is He Like?

22 China Crisis – African And White

23 Siouxsie and the Banshees – Slow Dive

24 Aztec Camera – Pillar To Post

25 Cure – The Hanging Garden

26 Clash – Should I Stay Or Should I Go?

27 Clash – Know Your Rights

28 Cure – The Figurehead

29 Psychedelic Furs – Love My Way

30 Simple Minds – Promised You A Miracle

31 Redskins – Peasant Army

32 Simple Minds – Someone Somewhere (In Summertime)

33 Cure – A Strange Day

34 Blancmange – Living On The Ceiling

35 Blancmange – Feel Me

36 Musical Youth – Pass The Dutchie

37 Cocteau Twins – Wax and Wane

38 Serious Drinking – Love On The Terraces

39 Jam – The Bitterest Pill (I Ever Had To Swallow)

40 Clash – Rock The Casbah

41 Passage – Xoyo

42 Chameleons – In Shreds

43 Weekend – A View From Her Room

44 Shambeko! Say Wah! – Remember

45 Simple Minds – Glittering Prize

46 Bauhaus – Third Uncle

47 Higsons – Conspiracy

48 Action Pact – Suicide Bag

49 Siouxsie and the Banshees – Melt

50 Farmer's Boys – I Think I Need Help

51 Stranglers – Strange Little Girl

52 Josef K – The Missionary

53 Gregory Isaacs – Night Nurse

54 Everything But The Girl – Night And Day

55 Associates – Club Country

56 Stranglers – Golden Brown

57 Theatre of Hate – The Hop

58 Fall – Look/Know

59 Captain Sensible – Happy Talk

60 Yazoo – Don't Go

Festive Fifty 1982

(Part 2 – all-time favourites)

1 Sex Pistols – Anarchy In The UK

2 Joy Division – Atmosphere

3 Joy Division – Love Will Tear Us Apart

4 Joy Division – New Dawn Fades

5 Cure – A Forest

6 New Order – Ceremony

7 Joy Division – Decades

8 Undertones – Teenage Kicks

9 Bauhaus – Bela Lugosi's Dead

10 Clash – White Man In Hammersmith Palais

11 Jam – Down In The Tube Station At Midnight

12 Joy Division – Dead Souls

13 Damned – New Rose

14 Dead Kennedys – Holiday In Cambodia

15 Siouxsie and the Banshees – Israel

16 Stiff Little Fingers – Alternative Ulster

17 Jam – Going Underground

18 New Order – Temptation

19 Clash – Complete Control
20 Public Image Ltd – Public Image
21 Altered Images – Dead Pop Stars
22 Echo and the Bunnymen – Over The Wall
23 Joy Division – Twenty-Four Hours
24 Only Ones – Another Girl, Another Planet
25 Sex Pistols – God Save The Queen
26 Joy Division – Transmission
27 Scritti Politti – The Sweetest Girl
28 Birthday Party – Release The Bats
29 Stiff Little Fingers – Johnny Was
30 New Order – Procession
31 Stiff Little Fingers – Suspect Device
32 Killing Joke – Requiem
33 Theatre of Hate – Legion
34 Killing Joke – Psyche
35 Ruts – In A Rut
36 Undertones – Get Over You
37 Sex Pistols – Holidays In The Sun
38 Joy Division – Isolation
39 Siouxsie and the Banshees – Jigsaw Feeling
40 Clash – Armagideon Time
41 Joy Division – She's Lost Control
42 Siouxsie and the Banshees – Switch
43 Specials – Ghost Town
44 Sex Pistols – Pretty Vacant
45 Siouxsie and the Banshees – Icon
46 Siouxsie and the Banshees – Hong Kong Garden
47 Magazine – Shot By Both Sides
48 Joy Division – The Eternal
49 Laurie Anderson – O Superman
50 Damned – Love Song

Festive Fifty 1983

1 New Order – Blue Monday
2 Smiths – This Charming Man
3 New Order – Age Of Consent
4 This Mortal Coil – Song To The Siren
5 Cocteau Twins – Musette And Drums
6 Smiths – Reel Around The Fountain
7 Billy Bragg – A New England
8 Fall – Eat Y'self Fitter
9 Smiths – Hand In Glove
10 Naturalites and the Mystics – Picture On The Wall
11 Red Guitars – Good Technology
12 Public Image Ltd – This Is Not A Love Song
13 X-Mal Deutschland – Incubus Succubus
14 Cocteau Twins – Sugar Hiccup
15 Cure – Lovecats
16 Cocteau Twins – From The Flagstones
17 Echo and the Bunnymen – Never Stop
18 New Order – Your Silent Face
19 Sisters of Mercy – Temple Of Love
20 Siouxsie and the Banshees – Dear Prudence
21 Fall – The Man Whose Head Expanded
22 Echo and the Bunnymen – The Cutter
23 Assembly – Never Never

24 Imposter – Pills And Soap
25 New Order – Leave Me Alone
26 10,000 Maniacs – My Mother The War
27 Sisters of Mercy – Alice
28 Cocteau Twins – Peppermint Pig
29 Aztec Camera – Oblivious
30 Redskins – Lean On Me
31 Chameleons – Second Skin
32 X-Mal Deutschland – Qual
33 Smiths – Handsome Devil
34 Tools You Can Trust – Working And Shopping
35 Fall – Kicker Conspiracy
36 Luddites – Doppelganger
37 Sophie and Peter Johnston – Television/Satellite
38 Cocteau Twins – Hitherto
39 S. P. K. – Metal Dance
40 Fall – Wings
41 U2 – New Years Day
42 Danse Society – Somewhere
43 Birthday Party – Deep In The Woods
44 Cabaret Voltaire – Fascination
45 New Order – The Village
46 Birthday Party – Sonny's Burning
47 Strawberry Switchblade – Trees and Flowers
48 Elvis Costello – Shipbuilding
49 Cure – The Walk
50 Tom Robinson – War Baby

Festive Fifty 1984

1 Smiths – How Soon Is Now?
2 Cocteau Twins – Pearly Dewdrops Drop
3 Men They Couldn't Hang – Green Fields Of France
4 Cocteau Twins – Spangle Maker
5 Mighty Wah! – Come Back
6 Membranes – Spike Milligan's Tape Recorder
7 New Order – Thieves Like Us
8 Sisters of Mercy – Walk Away
9 Fall – Lay Of The Land
10 Redskins – Keep On Keepin' On
11 Nick Cave and the Bad Seeds – Saint Huck
12 New Order – Lonesome Tonight
13 Billy Bragg – Between The Wars
14 Smiths – Nowhere Fast
15 Sisters of Mercy – Emma
16 Cocteau Twins – Ivo
17 Smiths – What Difference Does It Make?
18 Fall – Creep
19 Echo and the Bunnymen – The Killing Moon
20 New Order – Murder
21 This Mortal Coil – Kangaroo
22 Cocteau Twins – Donimo
23 Smiths – William, It Was Really Nothing
24 Smiths – Heaven Knows I'm Miserable Now
25 Frankie Goes To Hollywood – Two Tribes
26 Unknown Cases – Masimbabele
27 Very Things – The Bushes Scream While My Daddy Prunes
28 Smiths – Please Please Please Let Me Get What I Want
29 Billy Bragg – The Saturday Boy
30 Cult – Spiritwalker
31 Propaganda – Dr Mabuse
32 Yeah Yeah Noh – Bias Binding
33 This Mortal Coil – Another Day
34 Berntholer – My Suitor
35 Robert Wyatt – Biko

36 Smiths – Reel Around The Fountain
37 Jesus and Mary Chain – Upside Down
38 Cocteau Twins – Pandora
39 Flesh For Lulu – Subterraneans
40 Cocteau Twins – Beatrix
41 Special AKA – Free Nelson Mandela
42 Frank Chickens – Blue Canary
43 New Model Army – Vengeance
44 Fall – No Bulbs
45 Pogues – Dark Streets Of London
46 Hard Corps – Dirty
47 Echo and the Bunnymen – Thorn Of Crowns
48 Bronski Beat – Small Town Boy
49 Cocteau Twins – Pepper Tree
50 Working Week – Venceramos

Festive Fifty 1985

(another bumper list of favourites)

1 Jesus and Mary Chain – Never Understand
2 Jesus and Mary Chain – Just Like Honey
3 Fall – Cruiser's Creek
4 Cult – She Sells Sanctuary
5 Cocteau Twins – Aikea-Guinea
6 Chumbawamba – Revolution
7 Felt – Primitive Painters
8 Smiths – The Boy With The Thorn In His Side
9 New Order – Perfect Kiss
10 Housemartins – Flag Day
11 Men They Couldn't Hang – Ironmasters
12 Jesus and Mary Chain – You Trip Me Up

13 Pogues – Sally Maclennane
14 Three Johns – Death Of The European
15 Wedding Present – Go Out And Get 'Em Boy!
16 New Order – Love Vigilantes
17 Shop Assistants – All That Ever Mattered
18 New Order – Sub-Culture
19 Woodentops – Move Me
20 Pogues – A Pair Of Brown Eyes
21 Echo and the Bunnymen – Bring On The Dancing Horses
22 That Petrol Emotion – V2
23 Fall – Spoilt Victorian Child
24 New Order – Sunrise
25 Pogues – I'm A Man You Don't Meet Every Day
26 Rose of Avalanche – LA Rain
27 Cure – In Between Days
28 James – Hymn From A Village
29 Smiths – The Headmaster Ritual
30 Age of Chance – Motor City
31 Smiths – That Joke Isn't Funny Anymore
32 Smiths – Meat Is Murder
33 Fall – Gut Of The Quantifier
34 Beloved – 100 Words (session)
35 Nick Cave and the Bad Seeds – Tupelo
36 Sisters of Mercy – Marian
37 Vibes – I'm In Pittsburgh And It's Raining
38 Prefab Sprout – Faron Young (Truckin' Mix)
39 Fall – Couldn't Get Ahead
40 Billy Bragg – Between The Wars
41 Smiths – Well I Wonder
42 Fall – LA

43 Sisters of Mercy – Some Kind Of Stranger

44 Primal Scream – It Happens

45 New Order – Face Up

46 Hüsker Dü – Makes No Sense At All

47 Robert Wyatt – The Wind Of Change

48 Woodentops – Well Well Well

49 One Thousand Violins – Like One Thousand Violins

50 Shop Assistants – All Day Long

51 James – If Things Were Perfect

52 Del Amitri – Hammering Heart

53 Conflict – Mighty And Superior

54 Siouxsie and the Banshees – Cities In Dust

55 Fall – Rollin' Danny

56 Billy Bragg – Days Like This

57 Smiths – Barbarism Begins At Home

58 bIG fLAME – All The Irish (Must Go To Heaven)

59 10,000 Maniacs – Can't Ignore The Train

60 Cabaret Voltaire – I Want You

61 Smiths – Shakespeare's Sister

62 bIG fLAME – Man Of Few Syllables

63 Cocteau Twins – Quisquose

64 Pogues – And The Band Played Waltzing Matilda

65 Bogshed – Hand Me Down Father

66 New Model Army – No Rest

67 Cure – Close To Me

68 Triffids – Field Of Glass

69 10,000 Maniacs – Just As The Tide Was A-Flowing

70 That Petrol Emotion – Keen

Festive Fifty 1986

1 Smiths – There Is A Light That Never Goes Out

2 Age of Chance – Kiss

3 Fall – Mr Pharmacist

4 Primal Scream – Velocity Girl

5 Smiths – Panic

6 Smiths – I Know It's Over

7 Smiths – The Queen Is Dead

8 Shop Assistants – Safety Net

9 Jesus and Mary Chain – Some Candy Talking

10 Fall – US 80s–90s

11 Smiths – Ask

12 Smiths – Bigmouth Strikes Again

13 Weather Prophets – Almost Prayed

14 Half Man Half Biscuit – Trumpton Riots

15 Fall – Living Too Late

16 Wedding Present – Once More

17 Soup Dragons – Hang Ten!

18 Wedding Present – This Boy Can Wait

19 Bodines – Therese

20 Fall – Bournemouth Runner

21 Cocteau Twins – Love's Easy Tears

22 Primitives – Really Stupid

23 Pastels – Truck Train Tractor

24 Billy Bragg – Levi Stubbs' Tears

25 Soup Dragons – Whole Wide World

26 Fall – Realm Of Dusk

27 Age of Chance – Bible Of The Beats

28 Wedding Present – You Should Always Keep In Touch With Your Friends

29 That Petrol Emotion – It's A Good Thing

30 Very Things – This Is Motortown

31 We've Got A Fuzzbox – Rules And Regulations

32 The The – Heartland

33 Freiwillige Selbstokontrolle – I Wish I Could Sprechen Sie Deutsch

34 Mighty Lemon Drops – Like An Angel

35 Smiths – Cemetry Gates

36 Wedding Present – Felicity

37 Fall – Lucifer Over Lancashire

38 Cocteau Twins – Those Eyes, That Mouth

39 Half Man Half Biscuit – Dickie Davies' Eyes

40 Elvis Costello – I Want You

41 Billy Bragg – Greetings To The New Brunette

42 Flatmates – I Could Be In Heaven

43 Shop Assistants – I Don't Want To Be Friends With You

44 Mighty Mighty – Is There Anyone Out There?

45 Nick Cave and the Bad Seeds – By The Time I Get To Phoenix

46 Colourbox – The Official Colourbox World Cup Theme

47 Camper Van Beethoven – Take The Skinheads Bowling

48 Fall – Dktr Faustus

49 Mission – Serpent's Kiss

50 Pogues – The Body Of An American

Festive Fifty 1987

1 Sugarcubes – Birthday

2 Fall – Australians In Europe

3 Wedding Present – Everyone Thinks He Looks Daft

4 That Petrol Emotion – Big Decision

5 Smiths – Last Night I Dreamt Somebody Loved Me

6 Wedding Present – My Favourite Dress

7 New Order – True Faith

8 Wedding Present – A Million Miles

9 Fall – Hit The North

10 Wedding Present – Anyone Can Make A Mistake

11 I, Ludicrous – Preposterous Tales

12 Smiths – Stop Me If You Think You've Heard This One Before

13 Sonic Youth – Schizophrenia

14 Public Enemy – Rebel Without A Pause

15 Smiths – Girlfriend In A Coma

16 Jesus and Mary Chain – April Skies

17 Barmy Army – Sharp As A Needle

18 Big Black – Colombian Necktie

19 Primitives – Stop Killing Me

20 Cud – You Sexy Thing

21 Smiths – Paint A Vulgar Picture

22 Motorcycle Boy – Big Rock Candy Mountain

23 Smiths – Sweet And Tender Hooligan

24 Smiths – Half A Person

25 Smiths – Death Of A Disco Dancer

26 Fall – Athlete Cured

27 Eric B and Rakim – Paid In Full
28 Railway Children – Brighter
29 Smiths – I Won't Share You
30 Bhundu Boys – My Foolish Heart
31 Wedding Present – Getting Nowhere Fast
32 Prince – Sign O'The Times
33 James Taylor Quartet – Blow Up
34 Smiths – Sheila Take A Bow
35 McCarthy – Frans Hals
36 Eric B and Rakim – I Know You Got Soul
37 Sonic Youth – (I Got A) Catholic Block
38 Public Enemy – You're Gonna Get Yours
39 Jesus and Mary Chain – Kill Surf City
40 Smiths – I Started Something I Couldn't Finish
41 Jesus and Mary Chain – Nine Million Rainy Days
42 Big Black – L Dopa
43 New Order – 1963
44 Butthole Surfers – 22 Going On 23
45 Smiths – Shoplifters Of The World Unite
46 M/A/R/R/S – Pump Up The Volume
47 Colorblind James Experience – Considering A Move To Memphis
48 Gun Club – The Breaking Hands
49 Beatmaster/Cookie Crew – Rok Da House
50 Talulah Gosh – Talulah Gosh

Festive Fifty 1988

1 House of Love – Destroy The Heart
2 Wedding Present – Nobody's Twisting Your Arm
3 Jesus and Mary Chain – Sidewalking
4 Wedding Present – Take Me (I'm Yours)
5 Dinosaur Jr – Freak Scene
6 My Bloody Valentine – You Made Me Realise
7 Pixies – Gigantic
8 Wedding Present – Why Are You Being So Reasonable Now?
9 House of Love – Christine
10 Nick Cave and the Bad Seeds – The Mercy Seat
11 Inspiral Carpets – Keep The Circle Around
12 Morrissey – Everyday Is Like Sunday
13 Morrissey – Suedehead
14 Fall – Cab It Up
15 Wedding Present – I'm Not Always So Stupid
16 Fall – Bremen Nacht
17 My Bloody Valentine – Feed Me With Your Kiss
18 House of Love – Love In A Car
19 Sonic Youth – Teenage Riot
20 Sugarcubes – Deus
21 Robert Floyd and the New Four Seasons – Something Nice
22 Morrissey – Late Night Maudlin Street
23 Morrissey – Disappointed
24 Fall – Big New Prinz
25 Billy Bragg – Waiting For The Great Leap Forwards

26 Cocteau Twins – Carolyn's Fingers
27 Fall – Kurious Oranj
28 Overlord X – 14 Days In May
29 Sonic Youth – Silver Rocket
30 Pixies – Where Is My Mind
31 Mudhoney – Sweet Young Thing Ain't Sweet No More
32 Spit – Road Pizza
33 James – What For
34 Pooh Sticks – On Tape
35 Stump – Charlton Heston
36 Fall – Jerusalem
37 Shalawambe – Samora Machel
38 McCarthy – Should The Bible Be Banned
39 Pixies – River Euphrates
40 Fall – Guest Informant
41 Loop – Collision
42 Flatmates – Shimmer
43 Mega City 4 – Miles Apart
44 New Order – Fine Time
45 Pixies – Bone Machine
46 Primitives – Crash
47 Darling Buds – Shame On You
48 Happy Mondays – Wrote For Luck
49 Wedding Present – Don't Laugh
50 Public Enemy – Night Of The Living Baseheads

Festive Fifty 1989

1 Sundays – Can't Be Sure
2 Wedding Present – Kennedy
3 Pixies – Debaser
4 Happy Mondays – WFL
5 Pixies – Monkey Gone To Heaven
6 Stone Roses – I Am The Resurrection
7 Stone Roses – She Bangs The Drums
8 James – Sit Down
9 Inspiral Carpets – Joe
10 House Of Love – I Don't Know Why I Love You
11 Pale Saints – Sight Of You
12 Dinosaur Jr – Just Like Heaven
13 Jesus and Mary Chain – Blues From A Gun
14 Wedding Present – Take Me
15 Cud – Only A Prawn In Whitby
16 Mudhoney – You Got It (Keep It Outta My Face)
17 Stone Roses – Made Of Stone
18 Morrissey – Last Of The Famous International Playboys
19 Wedding Present – Brassneck
20 Morrissey – Ouija Board, Ouija Board
21 Inspiral Carpets – Find Out Why
22 808 State – Pacific State
23 Stone Roses – Fools Gold
24 Wedding Present – Bewitched
25 Pale Saints – She Rides The Waves
26 Field Mice – Sensitive
27 New Order – Vanishing Point
28 Birdland – Hollow Heart
29 Stone Roses – I Wanna Be Adored
30 Telescopes – Perfect Needle
31 Bob – Convenience
32 Jesus Jones – Info Freako
33 Spacemen 3 – Hypnotised
34 De La Soul – Eye Know
35 Inspiral Carpets – So This Is How It Feels
36 Pixies – Wave Of Mutilation
37 Pixies – Here Comes Your Man

38 Fall – Dead Beat Descendant
39 Dubsex – Swerve
40 Birdland – Paradise
41 Galaxie 500 – Don't Let Our Youth Go To Waste
42 Senseless Things – Too Much Kissing
43 Pixies – Dead
44 Snuff – Not Listening
45 Wedding Present – What Have I Said Now?
46 Popguns – Landslide
47 Morrissey – Interesting Drug
48 Family Cat – Tom Verlaine
49 Inspiral Carpets – Directing Traffik
50 Inspiral Carpets – She Comes In Fall

Festive Fifty 1990

1 Fall – Bill Is Dead
2 My Bloody Valentine – Soon
3 Ride – Dreams Burn Down
4 Ride – Like A Daydream
5 Sonic Youth – Tunic (Song For Karen)
6 Paris Angels – (All On You) Perfume
7 Wedding Present – Make Me Smile (Come Up And See Me)
8 Happy Mondays – Step On
9 Wedding Present – Corduroy
10 Orb – Loving You (session)
11 Teenage Fanclub – Everything Flows
12 Would-Be's – I'm Hardly Ever Wrong
13 Lemonheads – Different Drum
14 New Fast Automatic Daffodils – Big
15 Fall – White Lightning
16 Morrissey – November Spawned A Monster
17 Charlatans – The Only One I Know
18 Wedding Present – Don't Talk, Just Kiss
19 Nick Cave – The Ship Song
20 Wedding Present – Heather (session)
21 Boo Radleys – Kaleidoscope
22 Wedding Present – Crawl
23 Nirvana – Sliver
24 Pixies – The Happening
25 Ride – Taste
26 Ned's Atomic Dustbin – Kill Your Television
27 Lush – Sweetness And Light
28 Charlatans – Polar Bear
29 Dinosaur Jr – The Wagon
30 Fall – Blood Outta Stone
31 Pixies – Velouria
32 Happy Mondays – Kinky Afro
33 Fatima Mansions – Blues For Ceaucescu
34 Shamen – Pro-Gen
35 Fall – Telephone Thing
36 Sundays – Here's Where The Story Ends
37 Spiritualized – Any Way That You Want Me
38 Babes in Toyland – House
39 Wedding Present – Dalliance
40 Sonic Youth – Kool Thing
41 Fall – Chicago, Now!
42 Orb – Little Fluffy Clouds
43 Teenage Fanclub – God Knows It's True
44 Deee-Lite – Groove Is In The Heart

45 Bastro – Nothing Special
46 Farm – Stepping Stone
47 Farm – Groovy Train
48 Pixies – Allison
49 Pixies – Dig For Fire
50 Inspiral Carpets – Beast Inside

Festive Fifty 1991

1 Nirvana – Smells Like Teen Spirit
2 PJ Harvey – Dress
3 Curve – Ten Little Girls
4 Fall – Edinburgh Man
5 Teenage Fanclub – Star Sign
6 Teenage Fanclub – The Concept
7 Hole – Burn Black
8 Wedding Present – Dalliance
9 Fall – A Lot Of Wind
10 Hole – Teenage Whore
11 Primal Scream – Higher Than The Sun
12 Wedding Present – Dare
13 Gallon Drunk – Some Fools Mess
14 Wedding Present – Fleshworld
15 Catherine Wheel – Black Metallic
16 Nirvana – Drain You
17 Moose – Suzanne
18 Babes in Toyland – Hansel and Gretel
19 Boo Radleys – Finest Kiss
20 Slowdive – Catch The Breeze
21 Foreheads in a Fishtank – Happy Shopper
22 Wedding Present – Rotterdam
23 Slint – Good Morning, Captain
24 Fall – High Tension Line
25 Nirvana – Lithium
26 Pixies – Planet Of Sound

27 Smashing Pumpkins – Siva
28 70 Gwen Party – Auto Killer UK
29 Billy Bragg – Sexuality
30 Babes in Toyland – Catatonic
31 Babes in Toyland – Laugh My Head Off
32 Wedding Present – Octopussy
33 Chapterhouse – Pearl
34 Pavement – Summer Babe
35 Fall – The War Against Intelligence
36 Teenage Fanclub – Like A Virgin
37 My Bloody Valentine – To Here Knows Where
38 Curve – No Escape From Heaven
39 Babes in Toyland – Primus
40 Electronic – Get The Message
41 Fall – The Mixer
42 Babes in Toyland – Ripe
43 Fall – So What About It?
44 Th' Faith Healers – Gorgeous Blue Flower In My Garden
45 Field Mice – Missing The Moon
46 Pixies – Motorway To Roswell
47 Pixies – Bird Dream Of The Olympus Mons
48 Nirvana – Breed
49 Mercury Rev – Car Wash Hair
50 Bongwater – Nick Cave Doll

Festive Fifty 1992

1 Bang Bang Machine – Geek Love
2 PJ Harvey – Sheela-Na-Gig
3 Ministry – Jesus Built My Hotrod
4 Wedding Present – Come Play With Me
5 Fall – The Legend Of Xanadu

6 Fall – Free Range
7 Sonic Youth – Youth Against Fascism
8 Pavement – Trigger Cut
9 Babes in Toyland – Bruise Violets
10 Pavement – Here
11 Future Sound of London – Papua New Guinea
12 Fall – Ed's Babe
13 Jesus and Mary Chain – Reverence
14 Wedding Present – Flying Saucer
15 Suede – The Drowners
16 Sugar – Changes
17 Sonic Youth – Sugar Kane
18 Wedding Present – Silver Shorts
19 Wedding Present – Love Slave
20 Orb – Blue Room
21 Sugar – A Good Idea
22 Babes in Toyland – Hansel and Gretel
23 Sonic Youth – 100%
24 Wedding Present – Blue Eyes
25 Dr Devious – Cyber Dream
26 Sonic Youth – Theresa's Sound World
27 Pond – Young Splendour
28 Drop Nineteens – Wynnona
29 Datblygu – Popeth
30 Disposable Heroes of Hiphoprisy – The Language Of Violence
31 Frank and Walters – Happy Bus Man
32 Arcwelder – Favour
33 Therapy? – Teethgrinder
34 Fall – Kimble
35 Pavement – In The Mouth A Desert
36 Love Cup – Tearing Water
37 Pavement – Summer Babe

38 Disposable Heroes of Hiphoprisy – Television The Drug Of A Nation
39 Boo Radleys – Lazarus
40 Ride – Leave Them All Behind
41 Wedding Present – Sticky
42 Pavement – Circa 1762
43 Drag Racing Underground – On The Road Again
44 KLF and Extreme Noise Terror – 3AM Eternal
45 Buffalo Tom – Tailights Fade
46 Wedding Present – Falling
47 Pavement – Conduit For Sale
48 Sugar – Helpless
49 Verve – All In The Mind
50 Fall – The Birmingham School Of Business School

Festive Fifty 1993

1 Chumbawamba and Credit To The Nation – Enough Is Enough
2 Madder Rose – Swim
3 Huggy Bear – Her Jazz
4 PJ Harvey – Rid Of Me
5 Stereolab – French Disco
6 Voodoo Queens – Supermodel Superficial
7 Sebadoh – Soul And Fire
8 Breeders – Cannonball
9 Palace Brothers – Ohio River Boat Song
10 Eggs – Government Administrator
11 Fall – Why Are People Grudgeful?
12 Credit To The Nation and Chumbawamba – Hear No Bullshit

13 New Order – Regret
14 Pulp – Razzamatazz
15 PJ Harvey – 50ft Queenie
16 New Bad Things – You Suck
17 Cornershop – England's
 Dreaming
18 PJ Harvey – Wang Dang Doodle
19 Fall – Lost In Music
20 Fall – Glam Racket
21 Senser – Eject
22 Fall – I'm Going To Spain
23 Archers of Loaf – Web In Front
24 Credit To The Nation – Call It
 What You Want
25 Hole – Olympia
26 Fall – Service
27 Tindersticks – Raindrops
28 Chumbawamba – Timebomb
29 Fall – Ladybird (Green Grass)
30 Tindersticks – Marbles
31 Radiohead – Creep
32 PJ Harvey – Naked Cousin
33 Heavenly – At A Girl
34 J Church – Good Judge Of
 Character
35 Boo Radleys – Barney and Me
36 Madder Rose – Beautiful John
37 Tindersticks – City Sickness
38 Elastica – Stutter
39 Stereolab – Jenny Ondioline
40 Nirvana – Scentless Apprentice
41 Fall – A Past Gone Mad
42 Dinosaur Jr – Get Me
43 Fall – Behind The Counter
44 Madder Rose – Lights Go
 Down
45 Nirvana – Rape Me
46 Pulp – Lipgloss
47 Hole – Beautiful Son
48 Fall – It's A Curse

49 Trans Global Underground –
 Syrius B
50 Fall – War

Festive Fifty 1994

1 Inspiral Carpets (Featuring Mark
 E. Smith) – I Want You
2 Fall – Hey Student
3 Veruca Salt – Seether
4 Elastica – Connection
5 Supergrass – Caught By The
 Fuzz
6 LSG – Hearts
7 Elastica – Waking Up
8 Portishead – Sour Times
9 Stereolab – Ping Pong
10 Done Lying Down – Just A
 Misdemeanour
11 H Foundation – Laika
12 Ash – Jack Names The Planets
13 Pulp – Do You Remember The
 First Time?
14 Pavement – Range Life
15 Wedding Present – Swimming
 Pools Movie Stars
16 Sebadoh – Rebound
17 Hole – Miss World
18 Shellac – Crow
19 Madder Rose – The Car Song
20 Sleeper – Delicious
21 Pulp – Common People
22 Pavement – Gold Soundz
23 Pulp – Babies
24 Shellac – The Dog And Pony
 Show
25 Mazzy Star – Fade Into You
26 That Dog – One Summer Night
27 Nirvana – The Man Who Sold
 The World
28 Ash – Uncle Pat

29 Sabres of Paradise – Wilmot
30 Wedding Present – Click Click
31 Orbital – Are We Here (Industry Standard Mix)
32 Beck – Loser
33 Ash – Petrol
34 Pavement – Cut Your Hair
35 Madder Rose – Panic On
36 Salt Tank – Charged Up
37 Wedding Present – So Long Baby
38 Fall – City Dweller
39 Wedding Present – Spangle
40 Nirvana – Where Did You Sleep Last Night?
41 Fall – M5
42 Elastica – Line Up
43 Underworld – Dirty Epic
44 Nirvana – About A Girl
45 Hole – Doll Parts
46 ROC – Girl With A Crooked Eye
47 Sonic Youth – Superstar
48 Sleeper – Swallow
49 Tuscadero – Angel In A Half Shirt
50 Trans Global Underground – Taal Zaman

Festive Fifty 1995

1 Pulp – Common People
2 Pulp – Sorted For E's And Wizz
3 Wedding Present – Sucker
4 Ash – Girl From Mars
5 Dreadzone – Zion Youth
6 Ash – Kung Fu
7 Fall – Feeling Numb
8 Pulp – I-Spy
9 Dreadzone – Maximum
10 Long Fin Killie and Mark E. Smith – Heads Of Dead Surfers
11 PJ Harvey – Send His Love To Me
12 Pulp – Mis-Shapes
13 Supergrass – Alright
14 Zion Train – Dance Of Life
15 Bluetones – Bluetonic
16 Dreadzone – Fight The Power
17 PJ Harvey – Down By The Water
18 Catatonia – Bleed
19 Gorky's Zygotic Mynci – If Fingers Were Xylophones
20 Elastica – All Nighter
21 Bluetones – Slight Return
22 Tricky – Black Steel
23 Dreadzone – Little Britain
24 Fall – Don't Call Me Darling
25 Tindersticks – My Sister
26 Dick Dale – Nitro
27 Pulp – Disco 2000
28 Hole – Violet
29 Flaming Stars – Kiss Tomorrow Goodbye
30 Fall – Bonkers In Phoenix
31 Pulp – Underwear
32 Spare Snare – Bugs
33 Stereolab – Pop Quiz
34 PJ Harvey – To Bring You My Love
35 Dreadzone – Captain Dread
36 Cornershop – 6AM Jullander Shere
37 Billy Bragg – Northern Industrial Town
38 Van Basten – King Of The Death Posture
39 Solar Race – Not Here

40 Pavement – Father To A Sister Of Thought
41 Leftfield – Afro Left
42 Harvey's Rabbit – Is This What You Call Change?
43 Ash – Angel Interceptor
44 Dose (with Mark E. Smith) – Plug Myself In
45 Garbage – Vow
46 Dave Clarke – Red Three
47 Bis – School Disco
48 Dreadzone – Life, Love and Unity
49 Fall – The Joke
50 Safe Deposit – You Can't

Festive Fifty 1996

1 Kenickie – Come Out 2 Nite
2 Arab Strap – First Big Weekend
3 Delgados – Under Canvas Under Wraps
4 Kenickie – Punka
5 Underworld – Born Slippy
6 Fall – Cheetham Hill
7 Orbital – The Box
8 Gorky's Zygotic Mynci – Patio Song
9 Sweeney – Why?
10 Helen Love – Girl About Town
11 Stereolab – Cybele's Reverie
12 Billy Bragg – Brickbat
13 Fall – The Chiselers
14 Bis – Kandy Pop
15 Babybird – Goodnight
16 Fall – Hostile
17 Polly Harvey and John Parrish – That Was My Veil
18 Flaming Stars – 10 Feet Tall
19 Trembling Blue Stars – Abba On The Jukebox
20 Stereolab – Fluorescences
21 Tortoise – DJED
22 Jon Spencer Blues Explosion – 2 Kindsa Love
23 Polly Harvey and John Parrish – Taut
24 Quickspace – Friend
25 Dave Clarke – No One's Driving
26 AC Acoustics – Stunt Girl
27 Dick Dale – Nitrous
28 Belle and Sebastian – The State I'm In
29 Aphex Twin – Girl/Boy
30 Force and Stars – Fireworks
31 White Town – Your Woman
32 Zion Train – Babylon's Burning
33 Calvin Party – Lies, Lies And Government
34 Broadcast – The Book Lovers
35 DJ Shadow – Stem
36 Wedding Present – 2, 3, Go
37 The Prodigy – Firestarter
38 Ash – Oh Yeah
39 Placebo – Teenage Angst
40 Broadcast – Living Room
41 Tiger – The Race
42 Manic Street Preachers – A Design For Life
43 Half Man Half Biscuit – Paintball's Coming Home
44 Soul Bossa – Sore Loser
45 Urusei Yatsura – Kewpies Like Watermelon
46 Wedding Present – Go Man Go
47 Orbital – Out There Somewhere
48 Flaming Stars – The Face On The Bar Room Floor
49 Super Furry Animals – God Show Me Magic
50 Stereolab – Les Yper-Sound

Festive Fifty 1997

(only thirty-one tracks were broadcast)

1 Cornershop – Brimful Of Asha
2 Mogwai – New Paths To Helicon
3 Helen Love – Does Your Heart Go Boom?
4 Period Pains – Spice Girls (Who Do You Think You Are?)
5 Belle and Sebastian – Lazy Line Painted Jane
6 Novac – Rapunzel
7 Fall – Inch
8 Daft Punk – Rollin' And Scratchin'
9 Clinic – IPC Sub-Editors Dictate Our Youth
10 David Holmes – Don't Die Yet (Arab Strap Mix)
11 Blur – Song 2
12 Belle and Sebastian – Dog On Wheels
13 Hydroplane – Cross The Atlantic
14 Stereolab and Nurse With Wound – Simple Headphone Mind
15 Betty Davies and the Balconettes – Shergar
16 Arab Strap – Hey! Fever
17 Fall – I'm A Mummy
18 Spiritualized – Ladies And Gentlemen We Are Floating In Space
19 AC Acoustics – I Messiah Am Jailer
20 Stereolab – Fluorescences
21 Hitchers – Strachan
22 Bis – Sweetshop Avenger
23 Synchro Goldfish – Dandelion Milk Summer
24 Prolapse – Autocade
25 Dream City Film Club – If I Die, I Die
26 Stereolab – Mismodular
27 Delgados – Pull The Wires From The Wall
28 Propellerheads – Velvet Pants
29 Highbirds – Seventeen
30 Prolapse – Slash/Oblique
31 Angelica – Teenage Girl Crush

Festive Fifty 1998

1 Delgados – Pull The Wires From The Wall
2 Mogwai – Xmas Steps
3 Belle and Sebastian – The Boy With The Arab Strap
4 Ten Benson – The Claw
5 Tuesday – Unworldly
6 Cuban Boys – Oh My God They Killed Kenny
7 Bis – Eurodisco
8 Pulp – This Is Hardcore
9 Delgados – Everything Goes Around The Water
10 Helen Love – Long Live The UK Music Scene
11 Jesus and Mary Chain – Cracking Up
12 Daniel Johnstone – Dream Scream
13 Clinic – Cement Mixer
14 Badly Drawn Boy – I Need A Sign
15 Cinerama – Kerry Kerry
16 Plone – Plock
17 Laugmentasian – Soleil
18 Boards Of Canada – Aquarius

19 Solex – Solex All Lickety Spit

20 Evolution Control Committee – Copyright Violation For The Nation

21 Massive Attack – Teardrop

22 Spiritualized – Oh Happy Day

23 Solex – One Louder Solex

24 Mellis – Lemming, Chameleon Of Feelings

25 Half Man Half Biscuit – Turn A Blind Eye

26 Belle and Sebastian – Sleep The Clock Around

27 Clinic – Monkey On Your Back

28 Fatboy Slim – Rockafeller Skank

29 Super Furry Animals – Ice Hockey Hair

30 Billy Bragg – Way Over Yonder In The Minor Key

31 Freed Unit – Widdershins

32 Male Nurse – My Own Private Patrick Swayze

33 Mercury Rev – Goddess On A Highway

34 Elbow – Powder Blue

35 Gorky's Zygotic Mynci – Sweet Johnny

36 Gorky's Zygotic Mynci – Hush The Warmth

37 Melt Banana – Stimulus For Revolting Virus

38 Delgados – The Actress

39 Quickspace – If I Were A Carpenter (session)

40 60ft Dolls – Alison's Room

41 Boards of Canada – Roygbiv

42 Derrero – Radar Intruder

43 Hefner – Pull Yourself Together

44 Rooney – Went To Town

45 Soda Stream – Turnstyle

46 Sportique – Kids Are Solid Gold

47 Ten Benson – Evil Heat

48 Autechre – Fold 4 Wrap 5

49 Fall – Shake Off (session)

50 PJ Harvey – Is This Desire?

Festive Fifty 1999

1 Cuban Boys – Cognoscenti Vs Intelligentsia

2 Hefner – Hymn For The Cigarettes

3 Hefner – Hymn For The Alcohol

4 Fall – Touch Sensitive

5 Gorky's Zygotic Mynci – Spanish Dance Troupe

6 Elastica with Mark E Smith – How He Wrote Elastica Man

7 Fall – F-'Oldin' Money

8 Flaming Lips – Race For The Prize

9 Murry the Hump – Thrown Like A Stone

10 Low – Immune

11 Half Man Half Biscuit – Look Dad No Tunes

12 Flaming Lips – Waiting For A Superman

13 Cinerama – Pacific

14 Mogwai – Cody

15 Orbital – Style

16 Sonic Subjunkies – Do You Even Know Who You Are?

17 Super Furry Animals – Fire In My Heart

18 Cinerama – King's Cross

19 Salako – Look Left

20 Clinic – The Second Line

21 Godspeed You Black Emperor!
 – Hungover As The Oven At
 Maida Vale (session)
22 Hefner – I Stole A Bride
23 Bonnie Prince Billy – I See A
 Darkness
24 Super Furry Animals – Northern
 Lites
25 Mogwai – Stanley Kubrick
26 Kraken – Side Effects
27 Super Furry Animals – Turning
 Tide
28 Cuban Boys – Flossie's Alarming
 Clock
29 Dawn of the Replicants –
 Science Fiction Freak
30 Half Man Half Biscuit –
 24 Hour Garage People (session)
31 Pavement – Major Leagues
32 Hefner – I Took Her Love For
 Granted
33 Gene – As Good As It Gets
34 Plone – Be Rude To Your School
35 Smog – Cold Blooded Old
 Times
36 Broadcast – Echoes Answer
37 Add N To X – Metal Finger In
 My Body
38 Melt Banana – Plot In A Pot
39 Atari Teenage Riot – Revolution
 Action
40 Blur – Tender
41 Badly Drawn Boy – Once
 Around The Block
42 Aphex Twin – Windowlicker
43 Six By Seven – Helden
44 Appliance – Food Music
45 Pavement – Carrot Rope
46 Stereolab – The Free Design

47 Marine Research – Parallel
 Horizontal
48 Miss Mend – Living City Plan
49 Hefner – Hymn For The Things
 We Didn't Do
50 Wheat – Don't I Hold You

Festive Fifty 2000

1 Neko Case and Her Boyfriends
 – Twist The Knife
2 PJ Harvey – Good Fortune
3 Fall – Dr Buck's Letter
4 And You Will Know Us By The
 Trail Of Dead – Mistakes And
 Regrets
5 Broadcast – Come On Let's Go
6 PJ Harvey – Big Exit
7 Hefner – The Greedy Ugly
 People
8 Schneider TM – The Light 3000
9 Delgados – No Danger
10 Delgados – American Trilogy
11 Low – Dinosaur Act
12 Hefner – The Day That Thatcher
 Dies
13 Ballboy – I Hate Scotland
14 Delgados – Accused Of Stealing
15 Hefner – Good Fruit
16 Cinerama – Your Charms
17 Cinerama – Wow
18 PJ Harvey – Mess We're In
19 Shellac – Prayer To God
20 Boards of Canada – In A
 Beautiful Place Out In The
 Country
21 Laura Cantrell – Somewhere
 Some Night
22 Calexico – Ballad Of Cable
 Hogue
23 Fall – Two Librans

John Peel's Festive Fifties

24 PJ Harvey – Whore's Hustle, Hustler's Whore
25 Radiohead – Kid A
26 New Order – Brutal
27 Laura Cantrell – Two Seconds
28 Clinic – The Second Line
29 Cuban Boys – Vinyl Countdown
30 Cowcube – Popping Song
31 Herman Dune – Drug Dealer In The Park
32 Half Man Half Biscuit – 24 Hour Garage People
33 Cat Power – Wonderwall (session)
34 Cuban Boys – Theme From Prim And Proper
35 Lab 4 – Candyman
36 Gorky's Zygotic Mynci – Fresher Than The Sweetness In Water
37 Half Man Half Biscuit – Irk The Purists
38 Delgados – Witness
39 Mighty Math – Soul Boy
40 Smog – Dress Sexy At My Funeral
41 Cinerama – Manhattan
42 Laura Cantrell – Queen Of The Coast
43 Fall – WB
44 Hefner – Painting And Kissing
45 Orbital and Angelo Badalamenti – Beached
46 Bonnie Prince Billy – Little Boy Blue
47 Sigur Ros – Svefn G Englar
48 Radiohead – Idiotique
49 Belle and Sebastian – Fought In A War
50 Grandaddy – Crystal Lake

Festive Fifty 2001

1 Melys – Chinese Whispers
2 White Stripes – Hotel Yorba
3 Cinerama – Health And Efficiency
4 Bearsuit – Hey Charlie, Hey Chuck
5 Strokes – Last Night
6 White Stripes – Fell In Love With A Girl
7 Strokes – Hard To Explain
8 Camera Obscura – Eighties Fan
9 New Order – Crystal
10 Mogwai – My Father The King
11 Meanwhile, Back In Communist Russia – Morning After Pill
12 Saloon – Impact
13 Half Man Half Biscuit – Bob Wilson Anchorman
14 Miss Black America – Human Punk
15 Detroit Cobras – Shout Bama Lama
16 Half Man Half Biscuit – Vatican Broadside
17 Belle and Sebastian – Jonathan David
18 Strokes – The Modern Age
19 Pulp – Sunrise
20 Squarepusher – My Red Hot Car
21 Super Furry Animals – Rings Around The World
22 Mogwai – Two Rights Make One Wrong
23 Cuban Boys – Drink, Drink, Drink
24 Greenskeepers – Low and Sweet
25 White Stripes – Dead Leaves And The Dirty Ground

26 Ballboy – They'll Hang Flags From Cranes

27 Lift To Experience – These Are The Days

28 Strokes – New York City Cops

29 Pulp – Trees

30 Fall – I Wake Up In The City

31 Hefner – Alan Bean

32 Belle and Sebastian – I'm Waking Up To Us

33 Ikara Colt – One Note

34 Cinerama – Superman

35 Melys – I Don't Believe In You

36 PJ Harvey – This Is Love

37 Seedling – Sensational Vacuum

38 Antihero – Who's Looking Out For Number One?

39 Lift To Experience – Falling From Cloud Nine

40 Radiohead – The Pyramid Song

41 Ballboy – I've Got Pictures Of You In Your Underwear

42 Miss Black America – Don't Speak My Mind

43 Shins – New Slang

44 Mercury Rev – Dark Is Rising

45 Stereolab – Captain Easychord

46 Strokes – Someday

47 Hives – Hate To Say I Told You So

48 Rock Of Travolta – Giant Robo

49 Saloon – Freefall

50 Pico – Chard

Festive Fifty 2002

1 Saloon – Girls Are The New Boys

2 Cinerama – Quick, Before It Melts

3 Miss Black America – Talk Hard

4 Nina Nastasia – Ugly Face

5 Antihero – Rolling Stones T-Shirt

6 M.A.S.S. – Hey Gravity

7 Laura Cantrell – Too Late For Tonight

8 Pinhole – So Over You

9 Mark E. Smith Vs Safe and Sound – Identify The Beat

10 Ballboy – All The Records On The Radio Are Shite

11 Miss Black America – Miss Black America

12 Yeah Yeah Yeahs – Bang

13 Cinerama – Careless

14 Half Man Half Biscuit – The Light At The End Of The Tunnel

15 White Stripes – Dead Leaves And The Dirty Ground

16 Low – In The Drugs

17 Asa-Chang and Junray – Hana

18 Low – Canada

19 Coin-Op – Democracies

20 Belle and Sebastian – You Send Me (live at Peel Acres)

21 Datsuns – In Love

22 Fall – Susan Vs Youthclub

23 Jeffrey Lewis – The Chelsea Hotel Oral Sex Song

24 Ballboy – Where Do The Nights Of Sleep Go? (When They Do Not Come To Me)

25 Cornershop – Staging The Plaguing Of The Raised Platform

26 Saloon – Have You Seen The Light?

27 White Stripes – Fell In Love With A Girl

28 Cranebuilders – Your Song

29 Delgados – Mr Blue Sky (session)

30 Bearsuit – Drinkink

31 Ladytron – Seventeen

32 Boom Bip and Dose One – Mannequin Trapdoor

33 Von Bondies – It Came From Japan

34 Wire – 99.9 (session)

35 Mclusky – Alan Is A Cowboy Killer

36 Low – (That's How You Sing) Amazing Grace

37 Antihero – You Got Nothing (session)

38 Half Man Half Biscuit – Breaking News

39 Cinerama – Cat Girl Tights

40 Mclusky – To Hell With Good Intentions

41 Burning Love Jumpsuit – Cheerleader

42 Interpol – Obstacle 1

43 Melys – So Good

44 Delgados – Coming In From The Cold

45 Miss Black America – Infinite Chinese Box

46 Eighties Matchbox B-Line Disaster – Celebrate Your Mother

47 D4 – Get Loose

48 Mum – Green Grass Of Tunnel

49 Aphrodisiacs – This Is A Campaign

50 Dawn Parade – The Hole In My Heart

Festive Fifty 2003

1 Cinerama – Don't Touch That Dial

2 Fall – Theme From Sparta F.C.

3 Mogwai – Hunted By A Freak

4 Undertones – Thrill Me

5 Bearsuit – Itsuko Got Married

6 Mogwai – Ratts Of The Capital

7 Half Man Half Biscuit – Tending The Wrong Grave For 23 Years

8 Crimea – Baby Boom

9 C.S.L.M. – John Peel Is Not Enough

10 White Stripes – 7 Nation Army

11 Belle and Sebastian – Step Into My Office, Baby

12 Melt Banana – Shield For Your Eyes

13 Nina Nastasia – You, Her And Me

14 Ballboy – The Sash My Father Wore

15 Vive Le Fete – Noir Desir

16 Sluts of Trust – Piece O'You

17 White Stripes – Black Math

18 Yeah Yeah Yeahs – Maps

19 Broken Family Band – At The Back Of The Chapel

20 Darkness Vs S.F.B. – I Believe In A Thing Called Love

21 Million Dead – I Am The Party

22 Undertones – Oh Please

23 Ballboy – I Gave Up My Eyes

24 Party of One – Shotgun Funeral

25 Futureheads – First Day

26 Fall – Green Eyed Loco Man

27 French – Porn Shoes

28 Half Man Half Biscuit – It Makes The Room Look Bigger

29 Architecture In Helsinki – The Owls Go

30 Camera Obscura – Suspended From Class

31 Amsterdam – Does This Train Stop On Merseyside?

32 Maher Shalal Hash Baz – Open Field

33 Neulander – Sex, God, Money

34 Black Keys – Have Love Will Travel

35 M.A.S.S. – Live A Little

36 French – Gabriel In The Airport

37 Radiohead – There, There

38 Ballboy – Born In The USA

39 Cat Power – Werewolf

40 Broadcast – Pendulum

41 Keys – Strength Of Strings

42 Golden Virgins – Renaissance Kids

43 Belle and Sebastian – Stay Loose

44 Hyper Kinako – Tokyo Invention Registration Office

45 Grandmaster Gareth – Dr Dre Buys A Pint Of Milk

46 Super Furry Animals – Slow Life

47 Camera Obscura – Keep It Clean

48 Blizzard Boys – Ain't No Stoppin' This

49 Freddy Fresh – You Can See The Paint

50 Vaults – I'm Going

Index

Index